SPORTS HEROES AND LEGENDS™

Annika Sorenstam

Read all of the books in this exciting,
action-packed biography series!

SPORTS HEROES AND LEGENDS™

Annika Sorenstam

by Dax Riner

Twenty-First Century Books/Minneapolis

Twenty-First Century Books
A division of Lerner Publishing Group, Inc.
241 First Avenue North
Minneapolis, MN 55401 U.S.A.

Website address: www.lernerbooks.com

Cover photograph:
© Darren Carroll/Icon SMI/CORBIS

Library of Congress Cataloging-in-Publication Data

Riner, Dax.
    Annika Sorenstam / by Dax Riner.
        p.   cm. —   (Sports heroes and legends)
    Includes bibliographical references and index.
    ISBN 978–0–8225–7160–5 (lib. bdg. : alk. paper)
    1. Sorenstam, Annika, 1970– —Juvenile literature. 2. Women golfers—
Sweden—Biography—Juvenile literature. 3. Golfers—Sweden—Biography—
Juvenile literature. I. Title.
    GV964.S63R56 2007
    796.352092—dc22 [B]   2006101192

Manufactured in the United States of America
1 2 3 4 5 6 – JR – 12 11 10 09 08 07

Contents

A Dream Come True

When Annika Sorenstam stepped onto the first tee of the 1995 U.S. Open in Colorado Springs, Colorado, she was ready to show she had what it took to be a champion. With the rugged peaks of the Rocky Mountains as a backdrop, the setting could not have been any more dramatic. The Broadmoor Golf Club's East Course was considered one of the most challenging in the nation. At 6,500 feet above sea level, it requires players to adjust their games. The high altitude and thin mountain air help the ball carry farther, and the narrow fairways demand precise tee shots. Players who falter have to deal with the thick, heavy rough. The lightning-quick greens are a test for even the best putters.

For the first two days, Annika conquered the difficult course. In the first round of the four-round tournament, she scored an impressive 67. By the end of the second round, played on Friday, she was alone atop the leader board. On Saturday, though, things took a bad turn. Annika struggled the entire round, missing fairways and putts alike. After completing eighteen holes, she had fallen into a tie for fourth place. Annika was five strokes behind leader Meg Mallon. Mallon was playing excellent golf and had tied the course record by shooting a 66. Annika looked like she would once again come up short in a bid for her first Ladies Professional Golf Association (LPGA) win. Annika remained confident, however. "I was in the company of women far more experienced in the majors [big competitions] than I," she said. "But one thing I had learned is always to play as if you've got a chance to win."

That chance came early on Sunday. Decked out in a black hat, shirt, bow, and her trademark wraparound sunglasses, Annika avoided the mistakes that young players often make. She had been a pro for only one year, but she—not Mallon—looked like the cool, calm veteran. First Mallon bogeyed the third hole, meaning she needed one shot more than par, or average. Then she hit her tee shot on par-three fourth into a pond and made a triple bogey (three strokes more than par).

By the time Annika reached the eighth hole, she was tied for first place. A flurry of three birdies gave her a three-stroke lead with four holes left. (A birdie is one stroke less than par.) The best of the birdies came on the 11th, when she hit her drive into the thick rough. Using her wedge (a club designed for high, short shots), Annika hit a fantastic shot. She tapped in the seven-foot birdie putt and appeared to be on her way to her first win on the LPGA Tour.

But suddenly, Annika's inexperience began to show. Leading an LPGA tournament was uncharted territory for the twenty-four-year-old Swede. With each hole, the pressure increased. "My hands were shaking on the putter and on all the shots on the back nine," she said. On the 15th tee, Annika hit her approach shot into a bunker (sand trap). She had trouble getting out of the sand. When she nervously missed an eight-foot putt and settled for bogey, her lead was down to two strokes.

The par-four 16th wasn't any easier. "It felt like every hole was 700 yards," Annika said. (The typical distance between the tee and the hole is 300 to 500 yards.) She reached the green in good shape but three-putted for another bogey. Her lead was down to a single stroke with two holes left. On the par-five 17th, she had more problems. Her third shot was too strong, and the ball landed in the rough behind the green. Annika appeared to be on her way to another bogey or worse. She knew if she was going to be a successful pro, she would have to make the tough shots at the toughest times. With a wedge in hand, Annika stepped to the ball. Her chip shot rose in the air, landed on the green, and rolled toward the cup. When the ball came to a stop, it was just five feet from the hole. Annika coolly sank the putt for par. The lead was still hers!

As a teenager, Annika had dreamed of winning the U.S. Open. The tournament had been her favorite ever since she'd watched fellow Swede Liselotte Neumann win it in 1988. As Annika stood at the 18th tee, she realized that her dream was close to coming true.

As the largest crowd in Women's U.S. Open history looked on, Annika sent her drive down the fairway. She followed up the drive with an excellent second shot. The ball came to rest on the green, thirty feet from the pin. Annika knocked the ball close to the hole and calmly tapped it in for par. The shy, reserved Swede walked into the clubhouse at two-under for the tournament. Mallon was still on the course, however, and was just a shot back. All Annika could do was wait.

Playing one group behind Annika, Mallon only needed a birdie to force a playoff. Her best chance came on the 17th. She'd birdied the hole in each of the first three rounds, and there was no reason to think she wouldn't do it again. Perhaps playing too cautiously, Mallon left herself with a difficult thirty-foot putt for a tie. She pushed the putt short and wide of the cup before finishing the hole with a par. Annika's hopes for a U.S. Open championship would come down to Mallon's final hole.

Annika watched nervously from the NBC television booth as Mallon's drive landed on the fairway. A good chip shot to the green left her with an uphill twenty-foot putt to force a playoff.

The crowd fell silent as Mallon approached the ball. "As I watched her take her putter back, my heart thumped as if it would explode," Annika later said. All eyes were on the ball as it rolled toward the cup. The ball finally came to rest a foot from the hole. Annika couldn't believe it. She'd just won her first LPGA tournament, and she'd done it at the U.S. Open!

Chapter One

A Swede
with a Dream

Annika Sorenstam was surrounded by golf even before her birth. Her mother, Gunilla, played golf while she was pregnant with Annika. Annika once claimed, "[I] picked up the rhythm of her swing before I was born." Although Annika didn't become seriously interested in golf until she was a teenager, she credits her sports-crazy family for helping develop her desire to achieve greatness.

Annika was born on October 9, 1970, in Bro, Sweden, a small town thirty miles from the city of Stockholm. Tom, her father, was a marketing executive at IBM. Gunilla worked for a bank. Both parents loved sports. Tom even built a game room in the basement of the family's three-bedroom house.

In 1973 Annika's sister Charlotta, was born. As the girls grew older, they made good use of the game room. They spent countless hours in the basement playing badminton and

Ping-Pong. Despite Stockholm's long, cold winters, the city was full of sports enthusiasts. Skiing, golf, and tennis were popular, and Tom and Gunilla enjoyed all three. Middle-class families could afford country clubs in Sweden, and the Sorenstams joined the Viksjo Golf Club.

 Stockholm is Sweden's capital and its largest city. It is on the country's east coast, where Lake Mälaren meets the Baltic Sea. The central part of Stockholm is made up of fourteen islands.

Annika and Charlotta would tag along when their parents played golf. A rivalry developed between the sisters. Each wanted to outdo the other at whatever game they were playing. But the intensity the sisters shared was all their own doing. Tom and Gunilla were casual athletes who never pushed their children into sports. "To my parents' credit, my first memories of golf have more to do with ice cream and pretend pony rides than with white-knuckle competition," Annika recalled.

While her parents played a round of golf, Annika would putt on the practice green. Although Annika liked golf, she found tennis far more exciting. At the time, Sweden's Björn Borg was dominating men's tennis. He was Annika's hero. She watched with awe in 1980 as Borg captured his fifth-straight win at Wimbledon, one of the most prestigious tournaments in tennis. Like Annika, Borg came from a middle-class background. His parents weren't rich, and he didn't grow up with his own tennis court. His success showed ten-year-old Annika that anyone could become a skilled athlete. All one needed was passion, hard work, and desire.

Annika had been attending tennis camp since she was five. Her dedication and natural athleticism paid off as she quickly rose through the amateur rankings. She was one of Stockholm's top-ten players in her age group. But while Annika was a very good player, she wasn't the dominating force she wanted to be. "My forehand [swing] was good, but my backhand weak. Everyone would play to my weakness. I didn't like that," she said. "In golf . . . you can make the weakness work for you. Not in tennis."

As a teenager, Annika was recruited for the Swedish National Ski Team. Her specialty was slalom. While she still loves to ski, she has since become an even bigger fan of snowboarding.

Knowing she would never be a masterful player like Borg hurt Annika's pride. If she couldn't be the best, what was the point? One day, Annika decided she was through with tennis. She tossed her racket into the back of a closet. She vowed never to play competitively again.

Tom was disappointed. He knew his oldest daughter was good at sports, but most of all, he wanted her to enjoy them. He didn't want to pressure Annika into doing something she didn't want to do. As it turned out, Annika loved sports too much to give up on them completely. She had always liked golf, so she decided to give the game her full attention.

The Bro-Balsta Golf Club was a twenty-minute drive from the Sorenstam home. The club was close enough that Annika and Charlotta could ride their bikes to the course. Soon, the sisters were at the club daily, working on their golf game or just hanging out. Annika spent many summer afternoons at Junior Corner, where kids could eat snacks and listen to music. At night, she and Charlotta earned money by picking up golf balls at the driving range. "We were paid about ten dollars a barrel to pick up thousands of balls, and it made our forearms strong," Annika said. She would often spend her earnings on equipment, such as gloves, balls, and clubs.

Golf is a difficult game, even for the most seasoned professionals. While Annika liked playing golf, she was still young and a bit immature. "It took me a while to fall in love with the game," she admitted. "Like everyone who begins to play seriously, I was often frustrated. I threw my share of tantrums." As with tennis, Annika was a good but not great player. At fifteen, she was shooting in the 90s for a typical eighteen-hole round—decent, but not spectacular. She was hardly a child prodigy like Tiger Woods of the United States.

Annika and Charlotta shared a set of Mizuno clubs. The odd-numbered clubs were Annika's, and the even-numbered clubs were Charlotta's.

Despite her troubles, Annika wasn't ready to give up on golf. She liked that the mind games opponents would use in tennis didn't work in golf. In golf, it was just her, her club, and the ball. Annika had a scientific mind. Golf was a wonderful outlet for this type of thinking. Annika could apply science to her swing and her putting. In many ways, it was the perfect game for her.

In all likelihood, Annika would never have become a great golfer without the help of the Swedish National Golf Federation. Annika had natural talent and the support of her parents. But these alone would not make her a world-class golfer. The federation held organized practices for junior golfers. Annika attended as many as she could. At the practices, professional golfers helped the younger golfers strengthen their games. The coaching wasn't all physical, however. The Swedes believed that success was achieved not only with the body but with the mind. And so youngsters were also taught the mental aspects of golf. They learned to control their emotions and to think through their approach to each hole. Those golfers who showed the most potential were encouraged to attend federation training camps.

GOLF TERMS

Back nine: the last nine holes of a round
Birdie: one stroke less than par
Bogey: one stroke more than par
Eagle: two strokes less than par
Fairway: the closely mowed part of a golf course between a tee and a green
Front nine: the first nine holes of a round
Green: the short-cut grass that surrounds a hole
Par: the number of strokes a good golfer should expect to need to get the ball from the tee into the cup

---

Annika was still a teenager. She wasn't sure what she wanted to do with her life. As her golfing skills continued improving, she thought that she might be able to make the game her life's work. But until she heard her father's advice one rainy night, she didn't realize how much commitment she would need to become a professional golfer.

"One evening, after a long day of play and practice, I called my father to pick me up," Annika recalled. "When he arrived, he looked silently out over the range, where a few juniors were hitting balls in the rain and dwindling light. On the ride home, my father said, 'You know, Annika, there are no shortcuts to success.'" Annika often thought about her father's words. She used them as motivation when she was feeling down, tired, or sorry for herself. If she wanted to be the best, she would have to work harder than everyone else. She devoted herself to golf like she had never done before. She began playing in national tournaments, not just local ones. In 1987, at the age of sixteen, Annika joined the Swedish National Team. The move was a big step for the young woman. It would bring her in contact with a key figure in her early development.

Henri Reis was one of the most famous coaches in Sweden. Annika had shown some promise, so Henri became her coach. He taught at a course close to the Sorenstams' home. Annika was able to meet with him once a week. Almost immediately, Annika began to improve. She credits Reis with encouraging her to try a move for which she is known. She turns her head toward the target just before she hits the ball. This helps her focus on exactly where she needs to hit it.

Annika's golf talent was still raw. Many of her teammates were better than she was, including Carin Koch, who would also go on to join the LPGA. Surrounded by so many skilled golfers, Annika was unsure of herself. She had the basic skills, but she lacked confidence. Extremely shy, she felt more at ease behind a computer than in front of a crowd on a golf course. Annika was so uncomfortable in front of people that she sometimes would miss putts on purpose so she wouldn't have to give a victory speech. "I thought the real reason for my three-putts—pure shyness—was my little secret. But some of the coaches were watching me and noticing my not-so-coincidental misses," she said.

 Carin Koch was another student of Henri Reis. Carin won the 1988 Swedish Girls Championship title. She later turned pro and became a top player on the LPGA Tour. She is also a member of the European Solheim Cup team. She and Annika remain close friends to this day.

The coaches soon made a rule that the runner-up would also have to give a speech. Annika figured as long as she would have to talk to a crowd, she might as well do it as a winner. At the next tournament, Annika came in first.

In 1988 another key figure entered Annika's life. Former pro Pia Nilsson returned to Sweden to direct the Swedish Golf Federation's women's program. The team—and especially Annika—flourished under Pia's tutelage. The team won the Junior European Championship.

After graduating from high school, Annika got a job answering phones in the Swedish Professional Golfer's Association (PGA) office. She planned on going to college in the fall but still wasn't sure which school she wanted to attend. All she knew was that she wanted to study chemical engineering.

That summer Annika was invited to take part in a collegiate tournament in Tokyo, Japan. She had played all over Europe but never in Asia. She happily accepted the invitation.

Chapter Two

Arizona Wildcat

At the tournament in Tokyo, nineteen-year-old Annika was matched up against a player from the University of Arizona. The Arizona coach, Kim Haddow, was impressed with Annika's golf game. When the round was over, Haddow asked the young Swede if she would be interested in a scholarship to Arizona. Annika excitedly accepted the offer.

Golf had allowed Annika to travel throughout Europe and even Asia. But she had never been away from home for very long. Going 6,000 miles to attend college was something altogether different. When Annika had to board the plane to the United States, she was understandably nervous.

Gunilla knew just what to say to calm her daughter's nerves. "My mother came to the rescue," Annika said. "Her last words as I boarded the plane were, 'Remember, Annika, it's as far to come back as it is to go over.' She was telling me I could always fly home." Annika felt much better. She knew she could always return to Sweden if things didn't work out in Arizona.

Golf Scoring

The goal of golf is to get the lowest score possible. Every swing counts as one stroke, whether it's a 300-yard drive or a two-foot putt. Each hole has a set par, which is the total number of strokes a good golfer should expect to take to finish the hole. Par for almost all golf holes is three, four, or five. A golfer who finishes under par for a hole takes fewer strokes than is expected. A golfer who finishes over par takes more strokes.

When Annika arrived in Tucson, Arizona, in August 1990, she felt as though she were in another world. "I didn't know where Arizona was," Annika said. "I arrived . . . and it was over 100 degrees. I've never been in that type of heat. . . . It was quite a culture shock."

The rugged Southwestern landscape was very different from Stockholm. But one thing was certain—the desert provided the perfect weather for golf. No longer would Annika have to use orange balls while playing in the snow, like she did back in Sweden.

Annika headed straight for campus to get settled in. She was assigned to a dormitory for freshman (first-year) students. Her roommate was Leta Lindley, who was also a member of the golf team. (Later, Leta also became a professional golfer.) Leta's parents took the girls shopping for dorm-room supplies. Though Annika had learned English after spending time in England as a girl, she was overwhelmed by her new environment. She struggled to remember the English words for items like *blanket* and *pillow*. The Lindley family was patient and understanding. Annika pointed to what she needed, and they reminded her of the English word.

Adjusting to a new place and a new language is challenging for anyone, but Annika handled it well. The most difficult part about college was living in a dorm. Annika turned twenty in October, meaning she was a couple of years older than most of her fellow freshmen. The university was known as a place where people liked to have fun, but Annika was focused on more serious matters. Between classes, studying, and practice, she had hardly any free time. But she didn't mind. "For me, the party began and ended on the [golf] course," she said.

In Sweden golf coaches had encouraged their students to think for themselves. The situation was different in the United States. Annika had the impression that the U.S. coaches had a rule for everything. From study time to practice, every aspect of her life was strictly scheduled. "Sometimes, I had to raise my hand just to go to the bathroom," she said. Annika was used to being independent. This new way of thinking was hard for her to get used to.

GOLF CLUBS

Golf clubs can be divided into three general categories: woods, irons, and putters. Woods are long and have large club heads. Golfers get their longest shots with woods (the longest-hitting wood is called a driver). Irons are shorter clubs with narrow, angled club faces. The higher the number of an iron, the greater the angle of the club face and the higher a shot will go. The lower the number of an iron, the farther the ball will travel. Sand wedges and other wedges are other types of irons. Putters are flat. They are used on the green for short, rolling shots.

Annika's circumstances soon improved, however. She was allowed to move out of the dorm and into her own apartment. Once the season started, Annika showed just how comfortable she was in her new country and her new way of life. Her game was getting stronger and stronger. Almost immediately, she was a force to be reckoned with.

Annika earned her first collegiate win at the Oregon Invitational, sharing top honors with teammate Debbie Parks. That season, Annika finished in the top ten in all but one event. Her greatest moment came in the 1991 National Collegiate Athletic Association (NCAA) championship, held at Ohio State University.

Annika's biggest competition at the tournament was Christy Erb, from the University of California, Los Angeles. Erb jumped out to an early lead after the first two rounds. But Annika's round of 70 (two strokes under par) on Friday moved her into a tie atop the leaderboard. Erb had started out well in the third round and was at even par after the first nine holes. But thanks to some shaky putting, she slipped to +3 (three strokes over par) on the back nine, setting up a showdown on Saturday.

In the final round, Annika played in a group an hour ahead of Erb. The twenty-year-old Swede's game wasn't as strong as it had been on Friday. She managed just three birdies and had five bogeys, finishing with a two-over-par 74. She had to wait to find out if her performance was good enough for the title.

Annika's mediocre day left the door open for Erb, but the UCLA Bruin couldn't seem to recover from her third-round difficulties. Her putting never came around, and she finished with a 75. Annika had won the NCAA championship by one stroke!

All told, Annika's freshman year was memorable. She was named an All-American (one of the best college golfers in the nation) and College Player of the Year. Not bad for a shy girl from Sweden who had been a so-so golfer only a few years before.

Annika loves math, science, and computers. She probably would have become an engineer had she not become a golfer. She keeps all her statistics on her laptop computer and spends hours analyzing them.

In Annika's sophomore year, the twenty-one-year-old again stormed through the golf season. In nine total events, she earned four victories and three second-place finishes. She was the 1992 Pacific Ten Conference (PAC-10) champion. All that remained was her attempt to defend her NCAA championship.

The 1992 NCAA championship took place at Arizona State University's Karsten Golf Course. Playing close to home, Annika was even better than she had been the year before. A four-under-par 68 in the second round gave her the lead, and after Friday's third round, she was three strokes up on second-place Vicki Goetze. Goetze played for the University of Georgia and was the top-rated golfer in the college ranks. More than halfway through the tournament, Annika seemed almost a sure bet to win her second-straight NCAA title. On Saturday, she shot a one-under 71. But Goetze played the round of her life that day. The Georgia Bulldog birdied the first hole and didn't look back. At the end of the final round, Goetze had seven birdies and eleven pars.

She'd shattered the NCAA record for the lowest round with a seven-under 65. Annika's finish at five strokes under par was fantastic. But this time, her score was only second best.

Annika had one more tournament to think about, however—the U.S. Women's Amateur. The U.S. Women's Amateur is the leading golf tournament for female amateur golfers. The winner is awarded a gold medal as well as the Robert Cox Cup. The trophy is named for Robert Cox, a member of Britian's Parliament and a golf course designer.

Several thousand women enter the event. The USGA holds sectional qualifying events to reduce the number of contestants to a more manageable number. The main tournament opens with two rounds of stroke play. In stroke play, players record the total number of strokes taken in the entire round of golf. The leading sixty-four players then compete in a one-on-one match play tournament. In match play, the unit of scoring is the hole. On each hole, the most that can be gained is one point. Golfers play as normal. The golfer with the lowest score on a given hole receives one point. If both golfers tie, then the hole is halved. Match play scores of a game in progress are kept with a running tally. At the start of a match, the score is all square, or tied. The score is then recorded in terms of one player's lead over the other player. The matches are played over eighteen holes except for the final, which takes place over thirty-six holes.

VICKI GOETZE

During Annika's college career, her biggest rival was Wisconsin-born Vicki Goetze. (She later married and became Vicki Goetze-Ackerman.) Goetze burst onto the amateur golfing scene in 1989 when, at age sixteen, she became the youngest winner of the U.S. Women's Amateur. In 1992 she enrolled at the University of Georgia. While Goetze got the better of Annika during their amateur days, she hasn't enjoyed the same level of professional success. She turned professional in 1993 but has never won an LPGA tournament.

Vicki Goetze, who'd defeated Annika for the NCAA championship, was the favorite. To pull an upset would be the perfect end to Annika's year. The stage was set for an upset after Annika and Goetze both made the final. The matchup was a fascinating contrast in styles. Annika's strength was her long game (tee shots and long approach shots), while Goetze excelled at pitching and putting. All day long, the pair battled back and forth. As the golfers made their way to the final tee, the match was all square. Annika had one hole to pay back Goetze for the loss she'd handed Annika at the NCAA championship.

Annika used a strong tee shot to set herself up nicely on the fairway. A water hazard lay in front of the green, but Annika wasn't concerned. As long as she hit the ball cleanly, she would easily clear the hazard.

Annika pulled a six-iron from her bag, lined up the shot, and let it rip. Immediately, her heart sank. She hadn't hit the ball cleanly. Annika's ball plopped into the water. The door was wide open for Goetze. Annika managed to salvage a bogey, but Goetze made par. Annika had lost the title by one hole.

Her sophomore year over, Annika took time to reflect. She enjoyed school, but as a collegiate golfer, she had nothing left to prove. She was disappointed by coming up short to Goetze twice, but Annika knew she had few challenges remaining at the college level. It was clear that her future was in golf. Her mind was made up. She would leave school and turn pro.

Chapter Three

On the Rise

Annika's first chance to play against the professionals of the LPGA came at the U.S. Open in the summer of 1992. Thanks to her runner-up finish in the U.S. Women's Amateur, the twenty-one-year-old Annika received an invitation to participate as an amateur (meaning she wouldn't earn money for her finish). The U.S. Open is perhaps the most prestigious of the LPGA's major tournaments. Annika's performance in the tournament would give her a good idea of how she stacked up with the best. She knew the competition would be stiff.

The U.S. Open took place at the Oakmont Country Club in Pennsylvania. Oakmont was a historic course and highly regarded throughout golf. Right away, Annika noticed the difference between the amateurs and the pros. "I was very impressed with the LPGA players," she said. "They dressed well, and had Tour golf bags and professional caddies." In college the players would sometimes fool around during practice. Not so with the pros. From the driving range to the putting greens, the players were all business. Everyone looked so serious! The full weight of Annika's decision to turn pro began to sink in. The LPGA was home to the most talented golfers in the world. To succeed on golf's biggest stage, Annika would have to think and act accordingly. Annika decided she would not let herself be intimidated—even when she was practicing just a few feet away from some of the biggest names on the Tour.

MAJORS

In golf the "majors" are the four most prestigious annual tournaments. In women's golf, tournaments defined as majors have changed over time. The last change came in 2001, after the du Maurier Classic, held in Canada, was discontinued. The LPGA replaced the du Maurier Classic with the British Open. As of 2007, the women's four majors are the Kraft Nabisco Championship, the LPGA Championship, the U.S. Open, and the British Open.

Annika played well at the U.S. Open, but she had hoped to do much better. Putting wasn't the strongest part of her game, and the fast greens didn't help matters. They seemed as slick as glass, making the ball difficult to control. In the end, she shot twenty-four strokes over par and tied for sixty-third place out of sixty-six golfers. Annika felt like professional glory was still a long way away.

Annika returned to Phoenix for the summer to work on her game. To join the Tour as a professional, she would need to earn her Tour card. To earn her Tour card, she would have to attend the LPGA's Qualifying School. The school was held in October. That gave Annika a few months to prepare.

Taking advantage of the sunny Arizona summer, Annika practiced nearly every day. She was determined to earn her card on her first try. Before she knew it, summer was gone.

The LPGA's Qualifying School was in Daytona Beach, Florida. For Annika, her time there was a complete blur. "I don't remember much about my rounds there—except for the suffocating pressure," she said. "It felt as if my future depended on every swing for four long days." When it was over, Annika had come close, but not close enough. She had missed earning her LPGA Tour card by a single stroke.

Annika was devastated. She had left school to turn pro, but now she wouldn't be able to join the pro Tour. "I was deeply disappointed and didn't know what this setback would mean for my career," she said. "The more I thought about it, though, the more I realized things happen for a reason."

To feel sorry for herself wasn't Annika's style. She began to think about her options. She knew that she still had a good chance to get her card later. She had come up just one stroke short, and that was on her first try. Annika decided that she would focus on the positives. This wasn't the end of her dream—it was just the beginning.

Annika wasn't quite ready for the LPGA. But that was all right. She might not appreciate what it meant to be a pro if it came too easily for her. This was just another challenge. She knew that one day she would be a member of the LPGA Tour. But first, she came to an important decision. Perhaps more comfortable surroundings would help her adjust to life as a professional golfer. Annika would return home to Europe, where she could play professionally and continue to work on her game.

Early in her career, Annika carried a memo pad with her while she golfed. She would keep track of her moods while playing. If she was angry or frustrated, she would look at the notebook. By seeing what she had been doing when she felt happier, she hoped to keep negative thoughts under control.

Before she headed back over the Atlantic Ocean, however, Annika got the opportunity to play a few more times with the LPGA players. Her strong finish in the U.S. Open had earned her invitations to three tournaments in the spring of 1993. Any experience on the pro Tour was a good thing, Annika reasoned. She jumped at the chance.

Annika didn't have to travel far for the first tournament. The PING/Welch's Championship was held at the Randolph North Golf Course in Tucson, Arizona. As an Arizona Wildcat, Annika had played the course numerous times. The familiarity helped put her mind at ease. She finished in thirty-eighth place and earned her first professional paycheck. The $2,000 wasn't all that much, but it was a start!

Next came the Standard Register PING, held near Phoenix on a course called Moon Valley. The desert was even more magical this time around. Annika shot a sparkling 66 in the second round and played well the entire weekend. She shot 11 under par overall, good enough for fourth place. Not bad for someone who hadn't even earned her Tour card yet!

When she was handed her check for $36,985, Annika couldn't believe her eyes. In one tournament, she had earned more than she'd ever earned in an entire year! The first thing she did was call her family in Sweden. Her parents were very proud.

In April, in her final tournament before leaving for Europe, Annika finished a respectable ninth at the Las Vegas LPGA in Nevada. Having completed her brief LPGA run with a pair of top-ten finishes, Annika knew she had made the right choice in turning pro.

In Europe Annika continued to thrive. She came in second four times. Annika felt confident that she was finally ready for the challenges of the LPGA. But first, she had to address the matter of that pesky Tour card. She would have to earn it before she could enter more LPGA tournaments.

In the fall of 1993, Annika returned to the LPGA Qualifying School in Florida. This time, she was confident and relaxed. She tied for twenty-eighth place—good enough to earn her card. At last, Annika was officially a member of the LPGA Tour.

Her first tournament came in February 1994 at the HealthSouth Palm Beach Classic in Florida. After her strong showings the year before, twenty-three-year-old Annika liked her chances. But she was reminded of how unpredictable the game of golf can be. On the first day of the tournament, she shot a three-over 75. It put her in a tough position. Annika would have to do much better in the second round if she wanted to make the cut. The cut in a tournament is typically the elimination of the lower half of a stroke-play field at the midpoint of a tournament. Only those players with the best scores "make the cut."

Unfortunately, Annika's second round was even worse than her first. She tried hard, but her round of 77 left her short of the cut. Annika's next tournament was also forgettable. She missed the cut again. Others might have let the disappointment affect them. But Annika used the difficulties as motivation. She knew she was good enough to play with the best. She just needed to focus harder and play up to her potential.

From late spring into summer, Annika's game was inconsistent. She finished in the top twenty several times, but other times she played poorly. Wanting to golf as much as possible, she continued to travel overseas. She fared much better in these tournaments. But Annika wouldn't be satisfied until she tasted victory on the LPGA Tour. In July her game began to blossom. At the PING/Welch's Championship, she was six strokes under par and tied for tenth place. It was by far her best showing of the season. Her dedication and determination were starting to pay off. In August she headed to England to participate in the British Open, one of the most distinguished tournaments in golf.

Because of Britian's unpredictable weather and difficult, rolling courses, the British Open is considered one of the toughest tournaments on the Tour. Displaying remarkable poise, Annika handled the tricky conditions at the Woburn Golf and Country Club with the self-assured grace of a veteran. Annika finished tied for second, behind fellow Swede Liselotte Neumann. The $41,693 check was the most Annika had ever earned as a pro. But most important, Annika had shown that she was one of the Tour's true up-and-coming talents.

Around that time, Annika's personal life also took a turn for the better. She began to date David Esch, whom she had met on the Moon Valley driving range. David worked for PING, a company that makes golf clubs. On their first date, they went to a professional hockey game. Both of them loved sports. It was a perfect match!

Back on U.S. soil, Annika rode the wave of confidence she'd felt after the British Open. Her best finish was a tie for sixth at the Safeco Classic at the Meridian Valley Country Club in Kent, Washington. But her game was coming together. At the end of the season, she had taken home more than $125,000.

When it came time for the LPGA to name its rookie of the year, there was no debate. Annika was easily the best first-year golfer of 1994.

Annika's excellent rookie season captured the attention of Mickey Walker of Europe's Solheim Cup team. The Solheim Cup was created by golf manufacturer Karsten Solheim. It pits top players from the United States and Europe against each other. In 1994 the cup was held at the Greenbrier Sporting Club in West Virginia. The European team had won the previous cup in 1992 and wanted to defend its title. Most of the women on the European team had needed to earn a set amount of points on the European Tour. But as captain, Walker could also handpick a few players. When she invited Annika to join the European squad, the young Swede happily accepted the offer.

Annika started off well in her first Solheim Cup action. In the first round, she was paired with fellow Swede Catrin Nilsmark. The duo upset veterans Beth Daniel and Meg Mallon, strengthening Europe's hopes for a repeat. But after their initial success, Annika and her teammates struggled. Annika lost her final two matches, and the United States steamrolled its way to a 13–7 win.

Despite her up-and-down showing at the Solheim Cup, Annika's game was improving. But she had yet to achieve something that was very important to her: a win on the LPGA

Tour. The new season couldn't come quickly enough for Annika. At last, in February 1995, she was back in action. With a year on the Tour under her belt, Annika enjoyed a relaxed confidence she hadn't had the year before. Her peace of mind was evident in the season's early events. In four out of the first five tournaments she entered, Annika finished in the top five.

SOLHEIM CUP

In 1990 Karsten and Louise Solheim created the Solheim Cup, an international competition for women. Played every two years, the Solheim Cup features the top European-born players from the European Tour and the top U.S.-born players from the LPGA competing in a format similar to the men's Ryder Cup. Players on both sides compete for points in their respective tour events to earn a spot on the team. The three-day competition is based on a points system in which golfers earn team points by winning individual and pairs matches.

Still, her first win was proving elusive. She came close in the PING/Welch's Championship, settling for a second-place tie. In April and May, she struggled through a small slump. But just as it had in the past, a return to Europe gave her a jump start.

She cruised to victories in Austria and Germany to get herself back on track.

Annika's game was improving just in time for the 1995 U.S. Open, where she finally earned her first Tour victory. When presented the trophy, Annika was overwhelmed. Never comfortable giving speeches, all she could manage to say was "thank you." In her press conference, the shy Swede fought back tears. She called her parents in Sweden to share the news. Tom and Gunilla had been watching the Open on television, but the satellite went out late in the final round. All they could do was listen to the audio feed and try to picture their daughter on the course.

Annika's improbable victory at the U.S. Open instantly made her a star. Everyone wanted to talk to her. People were calling to offer congratulations. Reporters were calling for interviews. Companies were calling to ask her to promote their products in advertisements. The attention would have been a lot for anyone to handle, let alone a twenty-four-year-old who had never known fame. While Annika had dreamed of winning the U.S. Open, she hadn't been prepared for all the demands that accompanied the win. She began feeling worn down and soon became sick with exhaustion. "I wasn't lying around thinking, 'Poor me.' I simply wasn't mentally prepared for such a big win," she said. For the next four days, Annika couldn't get out of bed. Luckily, David was by her side to help.

Annika slowly regained her physical health. Emotionally, however, she still felt tired. She took some time off from golf. Over the next couple of months, Annika did a lot of thinking. If she wanted to be the best in the world, she would have to deal with all the extra demands. She worked on preparing herself mentally for the attention that comes with being a star athlete. "Everything that came with winning was an annoyance [to Annika], but Annika is a problem solver," David said. "She had to figure out how to deal with so much success. She likes to make her world consistent."

In August Annika returned to competitive play at the British Open. Critics were waiting to see if her win in Colorado had been a fluke. Annika showed them her game was much more talent than luck. She finished tied for second. It was the second year in a row she had accomplished that feat and in one of golf's most difficult tournaments. Annika's confidence grew. She returned to the United States and continued her outstanding play. In September she crushed the field at the GHP Heartland Classic, winning by ten strokes.

The following week, at the first LPGA tournament held in South Korea, things weren't nearly as easy. Down three strokes entering the final round of the World Championship of Women's Golf, Annika patiently chipped away at the lead. After nine holes, she finally caught the leader, Laura Davies of England.

The twosome battled back and forth on the back nine, but neither could pull away. After eighteen holes, Annika and Davies were still tied. On the first extra hole, Annika stumbled. Perhaps trying to be too perfect, Annika sent her second shot wide of the green. Meanwhile, Davies hit a beautiful second shot. Her ball landed on the green, just twelve feet from the pin. Forty feet from the pin, Annika asked her caddie for a wedge. Annika knew she had nothing to lose, so she decided to be aggressive. Her chip shot landed on the green and rolled into the cup for a birdie. Clearly rattled, Davies missed her birdie. Annika had earned another victory, making her the top money winner on the women's Tour for the year.

❝There's a calmness about [Annika] you don't normally see in young players.❞

—GOLFING LEGEND NANCY LOPEZ

Annika earned a number of other major awards as well. Her dominating performance earned her the Rolex Player of the Year honors. She also took home the Vare Trophy, awarded to the player with the lowest scoring average. No European had ever won both honors in the same year. She was the first woman ever named World Player of the Year by *Golf World* magazine. Even her homeland got in on the act. Annika was named Sweden's Athlete of the Year.

The LPGA had not witnessed a player with Annika's talent in many years. After just two years on the Tour, she was rewriting the record book. But more important, Annika was bringing the spotlight back to women's golf. Even casual fans were noticing the young Swede's accomplishments. Annika was the brightest young star in the game.

Chapter Four

Ups and Downs

Golf was Annika's passion, but the game wasn't her only priority. Her family and her peace of mind were also very important to her. At the beginning of 1996, she took a couple of months off to reenergize and spend time with David. When she rejoined the Tour, Annika's game was as sharp as ever. At the Nabisco, the LPGA's first major of the season, Annika finished second. She slipped a bit at the LPGA Championship, coming in a distant fourteenth. But she wasn't worried. She carefully picked which tournaments to enter, wanting to get the most out of each experience. She also wanted to make sure she'd be in top condition by the time the U.S. Open rolled around in June.

In May David and Annika got engaged to be married. The timing couldn't have been better. Annika immediately felt more at peace, on and off the course. David often traveled with Annika. He helped her stay calm and focused.

The 1996 U.S. Open took place at the Pine Needles Golf Club in North Carolina. Annika's confidence was at an all-time high. The twenty-five-year-old also played like a champion. She was just one stroke back after the first round. By the close of the second round, she had moved into first. At the end of the day on Saturday, Annika held a three-stroke advantage. Fans were eager to see what she would do on Sunday.

Annika didn't disappoint. Focused and determined, she put on a show. "On Sunday, I entered that magical zone where every shot goes where you want it to go," she said.

In her quest to stay in top shape, Annika visits the gym five days a week during the off-season. While she's on the Tour, she goes three times a week. "Getting stronger has helped me reach my goals, and my goals keep me motivated to do things I don't always feel like doing," she said.

That day Annika played some of the best golf of her career. A birdie on the eighth hole pushed her lead to six strokes. On the 10th, she nailed a 35-foot putt for eagle. She birdied the 16th after her tee shot hit the pin. As the day wore on, the gallery (crowd) grew and grew.

Annika's parents were waiting by the 18th green as their daughter made her walk up the fairway. The ovation she received was deafening, but when it came time for Annika to putt, everyone was quiet. She made a par to close out a record-breaking performance. Her eight-under 272 was a U.S. Open record. Her nearest competition was Kris Tschetter, who finished six shots back. Not since 1980 had the margin of victory in the Open been so large.

A year earlier, Annika had eked out a close victory for a U.S. Open championship. She'd been helped by some lucky bounces and some poor play by other contenders. This time she proved beyond a doubt that she was the best female golfer in the world. Defending a major tournament title was one of golf's most challenging feats.

Unlike in 1995, Annika was ready for the spotlight. "I still get the butterflies on the first tee. I still get sweaty hands, and my heart pumps a lot going down the 18th," Annika said. "But I know what winning is all about now, and that's a feeling I like."

Late in the season, her game was still in top form. She shot a blistering 18-under to take the CoreStates Betsy King Classic in October. Later that month, she defended another crown with a win at the Samsung World Championship. Once again the LPGA money title was hers.

Annika's year had one dark spot, however. In the Solheim Cup, the European team blew a big lead against the United States. On the final day, Annika won her match against former college rival Wendy Ward, but her efforts weren't enough to hold off the U.S. team.

That setback couldn't erase the glow from what had been a remarkable season. When Annika pictured the future, she envisioned nothing but success. Who could doubt she would be winning major championships year-in, year-out for decades to come?

❝ We have a great friendship and one I certainly treasure because to see what she's doing out there, it's a lot of fun to watch.❞

—TIGER WOODS

Annika began 1997 on a happy note. She and David were married in January. Just one week later, Annika won the Chrysler-Plymouth Tournament of Champions. In February, she took the Hawaiian Ladies Open. In March she encountered her first disappointment. She finished tied for eighth in the season's first major, the Nabisco. But the following week, Annika enjoyed her third win of the season at the Longs Drugs Challenge, where she bested Pamela Kometani in a playoff. With a combination of grace under pressure and astounding consistency, Annika seemed almost unstoppable. She just needed to improve in the majors.

❝ *She hits it dead solid more consistently than any golfer I've ever seen.* **❞**

—ELY CALLAWAY, FOUNDER OF CALLAWAY GOLF

Annika's baffling struggles in the majors continued at the LPGA Championship in May. A final round 67 drew Annika within one shot of the lead, but she had to settle for third place. In June Annika bounced back at the Michelob Light Classic. Not even bad weather could slow down the twenty-six-year-old star. She conquered the rainy, windy conditions on her way to an eleven-under, three-stroke victory over Hiromi Kobayashi. Annika's favorite tournament, the U.S. Open, was just a month away. She seemed ready to defend her title once again.

The Women's U.S. Open was held at Pumpkin Ridge Golf Club near Portland, Oregon. If Annika could prevail, she would become the first golfer to win the tournament three consecutive times. But things didn't go as she'd hoped. In the first round, Annika struggled mightily. She never recovered from a disastrous triple bogey on the ninth hole, shooting a six-over-par 77. She did a little better the next day, firing a 73. But it wasn't good enough to make the cut. Fans had expected to watch Annika go for the record that weekend. They were shocked not to see her out on the course. "It just shows what a difficult game golf can be," Annika said. "I wasn't mentally ready that week and the course got me."

Three weeks later, her drought in the majors continued. She shot a four-over 77 in the second round of the du Maurier Classic to miss the cut.

 Annika's hobbies range from music and cooking to investing in real estate and stocks.

But true champions rise above their disappointments, and that's what Annika did. She slowly gained momentum, finishing third at the British Open in August and second at the Safeco Classic in September. At the CoreStates Betsy King Classic in October, Annika defended her title, taking a two-shot win over Kelly Robbins.

The season's final tournament came the weekend before Thanksgiving. Held at the Desert Inn Golf Club in Las Vegas, the LPGA Championship offered a chance for Annika to end the season on a high note.

Heading into the final round, Annika was nine strokes under par. Her two-under-70 day included pars on the final nine holes and moved her to –11. Crowd favorite and golfing legend Nancy Lopez hung close and was even tied for the lead after eight holes. But she soon faded, limping to the finish with a bogey and a double bogey to close out her round.

While Annika was making pars, however, Pat Hurst and Lorie Kane were making birdies. Hurst's 68 and Kane's 67 forced a three-way sudden-death playoff. In this form of overtime, the golfers play until they are no longer tied. On the first extra hole, Annika made yet another par, her tenth in a row. Hurst faltered with a bogey, and her day was done. After Kane made her par to stay alive, the play-off was down to a twosome. Both Kane and Annika made pars on the second playoff hole, but Kane then wilted under the pressure. The second-year pro missed a five-foot putt on the third hole for a bogey. Annika made par, and the title was hers. Once again she'd simply worn down her competition with her consistency.

As always Annika's competitors praised her. "[Annika is] the best we have and she's the best in the world," Kane said. "I've learned a lot from her."

The victory earned Annika Rolex Player of the Year honors and pushed her winnings to more than $1 million for the season. She barely missed out on the Vare Trophy, however. Karrie Webb, an up-and-comer from Australia, took home that award.

Chapter Five

Rising to the Challenge

As the 1990s came to a close, the calm and cool Annika Sorenstam was swiftly becoming a golfing icon. In the first four months of 1998, she entered nine tournaments and finished in the top ten in eight of them. The only time she didn't crack the top ten was in a major. At the LPGA Championship in June, she was +2 and tied for thirtieth. For some reason, she just couldn't get over the hump in the most prestigious tournaments.

In the final round of her next start, at the Michelob Light Classic, Annika was down two strokes to Donna Andrews with three holes to go. That was when Annika made her move. On the 16th hole, she nailed a nine-iron shot within twelve feet of the cup and then sank a birdie. She topped that shot on 18, hitting a spectacular eighty-yard wedge shot within two feet of the pin. The elevated green meant Annika couldn't see where her ball had ended up. But when the crowd erupted with a huge cheer, she knew her shot had been good. She knocked in the birdie to force a sudden-death playoff.

Annika and Andrews returned to the par-five 18th for the first extra hole. Because of the way the TV crew and cameras were set up, the 18th was the only hole that would be used in the playoff. After both players got pars, they played the hole again. "Annika looked at me after we'd played it once and said, 'We could be here all day, as consistent as you and I are,'" Andrews said.

Both players hit good drives and second shots. Andrews hit her approach shot twelve feet to the right of the hole. Annika's short game had been strong all tournament, and she repeated her earlier magic. Another beautiful iron shot came to rest just four feet from the cup. After Andrews missed her birdie putt, Annika sank hers and notched her first victory of the season.

 Annika won more LPGA tournaments—eighteen— than any other LPGA Tour player in the 1990s.

The following week, Annika earned her sixteenth career victory at the Safeco Classic and upped her overall winnings past the $3 million mark. But at the U.S. Open at the Blackwolf

Run Golf Club in Kohler, Wisconsin, the major curse continued. A third-round 79 killed any hopes she had for a late comeback, and a final-round 77 left her tied for forty-first, a distant twelve strokes back from the young South Korean star Se Ri Pak.

Annika's ability to rebound was beginning to be a pattern. Two weeks after her U.S. Open disaster, she headed to the Japanese Airlines Big Apple Classic at Wykagyl Country Club in New Rochelle, New York. The women's golf world was buzzing with talk of Pak, a twenty-year-old rookie. Fresh off her win at the Open, Pak was the center of media attention.

As usual, Annika did her talking with her clubs. She stormed to a six-stroke lead over Michelle Estill, following up a five-under 66 in the second round with a third-round 65. On Sunday, however, Annika got off to a bumpy start. Over the first four holes, she took two bogeys. While playing the sixth hole, she noticed her lead had shrunk to three strokes. She had to play better than that if she wanted to hold on to the lead. Annika then made three straight birdies to push her lead back to six at the turn (after nine holes). On the back nine, she got hot again, firing three birdies in four holes to ice the win. "She's playing a different game," said Joan Pitcock, whose late charge was far too little, too late. "She's afraid of nothing."

At the end of the day, Annika's –19 broke the tournament's scoring record. Her eight-stroke margin of victory was also a tournament record. Pak, who still was the focus of attention even when hopelessly behind, finished twenty-three strokes back, in forty-fourth place. "Se Ri deserves all the attention," Annika said graciously. "But I can play too."

The stunning win clinched Player of the Year honors for Annika. And the twenty-eight-year-old regained the Vare Trophy in impressive style, becoming the first player in LPGA history with a season average below 70.

❝[Annika is] a human golf machine. [She is] ahead of anyone in the game—male or female.❞

—PGA GOLFER JOHNNY MILLER

For any other golfer, Annika's 1999 season would have been a great success. She won twice and finished second four times. Her playoff victory over Tina Barrett in the Michelob Light Classic marked Annika's third-straight win at that tournament. Only five other women in the LPGA had ever won the same tournament three times in a row: Louise Suggs, Kathy Whitworth, Sandra Haynie, Karrie Webb, and Laura Davies. Another of Annika's season highlights came in the first round of the Sara Lee Classic. She fired a 61, the lowest first-round score in LPGA history.

The accomplishments were nice, but overall, 1999 was far below the high standards Annika had set for herself. The biggest disappointment was her failure to win a major. Her best finish was a tie for seventh at the Kraft Nabisco Championship. At the LPGA Championship, she tied for sixteenth place. Even worse, at the U.S. Open she missed the cut for the second time in three years. Annika just wasn't coming through in the LPGA's biggest events.

After she'd won her second U.S. Open, Annika had figured the victories would just keep coming. After the 1999 season, she took a long, hard look at her game. "I'd lost focus," she later admitted. "I'd already reached my biggest goals—Player of the Year, the Vare Trophy, two U.S. Open titles."

Another factor had been Annika's lack of a rival. Until 1999 she didn't have another player who would challenge her week in, week out. While she never needed any motivation beyond her own desire to be the best, sometimes Annika had trouble maintaining her intensity. "Lucky for me, Karrie Webb came along to give me a swift kick in the pants," Annika said.

At the decade's close, Webb mounted a serious challenge to Annika's claim of being the LPGA's best golfer. The young Australian had been playing well for several years. Even before she joined the Tour, Webb had raised eyebrows by winning the 1995 British Open. In 1997 she beat Annika for the Vare Trophy. But Webb's performance in 1999 really made everyone take notice. She won six tournaments that year, including one major—the du Maurier Classic. "I saw how [well] she was playing. I saw her results and figured that's what I want," Annika said.

In 2000 the rivalry heated up. Twenty-nine-year-old Annika was determined not to give up her hold on the title of "world's best female golfer" without a fight. The rivalry took center stage at the LPGA Takefuji Classic in March. But the result wasn't exactly what Annika had hoped. Proving that Annika wasn't the only player solid under pressure, Webb emerged victorious with a birdie on the first playoff hole. True to form, Annika shook off the loss. The following week, she defeated Pat Hurst in a sudden-death playoff at the Welch's/Circle K Championship. The win made her statistically eligible for the LPGA Tour Hall of Fame. In many sports, media members vote players into the hall of fame. But in the LPGA, golfers have to meet a series of requirements to be inducted. First, they must have either won a major championship or been awarded the Vare Trophy or Rolex Player of the Year. Annika had met that requirement with her first Tour victory at the U.S. Open. Second, LPGA members must also earn at least 27 points. Players on the Tour earn one point for an official tournament win, two points for a victory in a major, and one point for each Vare Trophy or Player of the Year honor. With her win at the

Welch's/Circle K Championship, Annika had earned the required number of points to get into the hall. But there was one last requirement she had not yet met. LPGA members must have been on the Tour for ten years. Annika would have to wait until 2003 to become a member of the LPGA Tour Hall of Fame.

KARRIE WEBB

Karrie Webb was born in Australia on December 21, 1974. She began her professional golf career in 1994 and joined the LPGA Tour in 1996. Webb, known for coming through in golf's biggest tournaments, has won all four current majors. She also won the du Maurier Classic when it was still considered a major. Like Annika, Webb qualified for the LPGA Tour Hall of Fame in 2000 but had to wait until she'd spent ten years on the Tour to be inducted.

In June Annika got her chance to put herself back on top. At the Evian Masters, she and Webb once again found themselves in a sudden-death playoff. Webb took the lead after the first round with a six-under 66. Annika was four shots back after shooting a 70. In the second and third rounds, Annika crept closer. Entering the final round, Annika had trailed Webb by just one shot. On Sunday the rivals headed to the 18th green tied for the lead. Annika made a birdie, but so did Webb. The pair headed back to the par-five 18th tee for the first playoff hole.

During the LPGA's fiftieth anniversary celebration in 2000, Annika was named one of the top fifty players in LPGA history. Others on the list include Amy Alcott, JoAnne Carner, Nancy Lopez, and Beth Daniel.

Annika stroked her tee shot down the middle of the fairway. Coolly, Webb answered with her own excellent drive. Both women were playing well. Annika knew she'd have to be aggressive if she wanted to win. She sent her second shot right at the pin. Her ball came to rest just six feet from the hole. Webb would have to hit an amazing shot to have any chance. But it was not to be. Her second shot went wide, sailing into a bunker beside the green. Annika made her eagle putt for the victory.

The duo gave women's golf a much-needed shot in the arm. The sport has always been most dynamic when two or more great players are battling it out to be the best. Webb didn't just push Annika to improve. She also helped make the game more exciting for fans.

Annika finished the year with five wins, including back-to-back victories at the Jamie Farr Kroger Classic and the Japan

Airlines Big Apple Classic. During the final round, the fans at the Big Apple Classic were treated to another great Annika moment.

CHARLOTTA SORENSTAM

Annika isn't the only professional golfer in the family. Her sister, Charlotta, followed her onto the LPGA and European Tours. Charlotta attended the University of Texas and joined the Tour in 1997. In 2000 she earned her first and only LPGA win at the Standard Register PING. In 2004 Charlotta was awarded the Mary Bea Porter Award for saving fellow golfer Donna Caponi from choking on an apple at the 2003 LPGA Championship. She lives in Scottsdale, Arizona.

After chasing fellow golfer Rosie Jones all day, Annika finally tied her on the 15th hole. The two women were still tied when they arrived at the 17th tee. Annika pulled her tee shot into the rough left of the fairway. When she got to her ball, she saw just how tough a shot she had. A large tree loomed in front of her. There was no way to hit over it. She could hit a low shot, but the fairways were extremely soft after several days of rain. To reach the green, Annika would have to hit the ball low enough to avoid the tree but hard enough to roll on the wet ground. After a discussion with her caddie, Terry McNamara, Annika chose a seven-iron. It was the perfect club. With just the right mix of strength and touch, Annika got the ball under the tree, across the fairway, and within fifteen feet of the cup. After such an amazing shot, there was no way Annika was going to lose. She made her birdie to take the lead, then made par on 18 for the win.

Despite Annika's strong season-ending run, Webb's seven wins kept her atop the money list. But most painful to Annika, the Australian star had shined brightest in the majors. In the four most prestigious tournaments on the Tour, Webb won two—the Kraft Nabisco and the U.S. Open—and finished in the top ten in the others. It seemed Webb was the new darling of the LPGA Tour.

Meanwhile, five years had passed since Annika had tasted victory in a major. She was eager to do something about it.

Chapter Six

Fifty-nine

When thirty-year-old Annika Sorenstam looked back at her 2000 season, one thing stood out: putting. Her putting average had been the worst of her career, good only for 122nd on the Tour. If she were going to compete with Webb, Annika needed to strengthen her game on the greens. "I figured, 'What is [Webb] better at?'" Annika said. "And I realized that she was making all the putts that I wasn't making. That was the difference."

For Annika, putting was just another challenge. She devoted an extra hour each day to the practice green. "I didn't alter my mechanics much," she said. "I just worked on speed and distance control. I would hit fifty to one hundred putts with my right hand only, and attempt to [hit] a dozen 30-footers to within a putter's length of the hole. If I missed, I had to start over." Annika looked up PGA Senior Tour golfer Dave Stockton for some more pointers. Soon her putting touch was back and better than ever.

Determined to improve strength and stamina, Annika hired a personal trainer. That winter she went through a rigorous physical regimen. She ran, swam, and did more than seven hundred sit-ups a day. She biked and kickboxed too. By the time February 2001 rolled around, Annika was in the best shape of her life.

---

66 *When she gets her game going, she's like a robot. She doesn't break down.* 99

—BETH DANIEL, LPGA GOLFING LEGEND

Just as important, the workouts had also helped Annika clear her mind. She refused to dwell on the negatives, focusing only the positives. In her first two events of the season, Annika came in second. In her next event, the Welch's/Circle K Championship, she won by six strokes. She finished an incredible 23 under par and shot under 70 in all four rounds. As spectacular as that performance was, Annika wasn't done yet.

The following week, at the Standard Register PING, Annika returned to familiar grounds. The Moon Valley Country Club in Phoenix was a special course for her. She had played there many times while in college. And it was where she had met her husband, David.

Annika's opening round was solid but uneventful. She gave little indication that the tournament would be anything special. The next morning, Annika headed back to Moon Valley. She went through her usual routine, putting, chipping, and hitting range balls for more than an hour. "There was nothing unusual about how I felt or hit the ball," she said.

Annika's early morning tee time gave her an advantage she planned to exploit. Since the harsh Arizona sun hadn't had time to dry out the grass, the course would be relatively soft. Annika could be more aggressive with her shots.

When on the green, the ball may be picked up if it needs to be cleaned or if it's in the way of an opponent's putting line. The ball's position must then be marked using a ball marker. A ball marker is usually a flat, round piece of plastic or a coin. Annika marks her balls on the green with a Ben Franklin half-dollar coin. A fan gave it to her.

When Annika was nineteen, Pia Nilsson, her Swedish National Team coach, had given her a document called

Vision54, which posed the idea that in one round, a player could birdie every hole on the golf course. Swedish players carried this idea with them when they stepped onto the golf course. *Vision54* was at the back of Annika's mind as she began her round at the 10th tee.

With her old coach and her father in the crowd and her sister, Charlotta, as a playing partner, Annika birdied her first hole. Then she birdied her second. On her third hole, Annika had a tough thirty-foot putt for a birdie. The cup was up and over a ridge, but Annika stroked it perfectly and it dropped into the cup. On her fourth hole, she had a chance for an eagle but settled for another birdie. She asked her caddie how many birdies she'd made. McNamara told her: four. "Well, I've done six in a row before," she said. "Let's keep going."

And keep going she did. Everything was working for her. Four more birdies gave her an incredible eight in a row. "I had a lot of thoughts in my head," she said. "I was trying to stay calm and hit good shots, trying to hit it straight every time."

The streak finally ended on the ninth hole. "It was kind of funny," said Meg Mallon, who was in Annika's threesome (group of three golfers) that day. "The first few holes, I was furious because I'm getting my butt kicked. Then, at the turn, it wasn't a matter of whether Annika was going to break 60. It was a matter of by how many."

Annika Sorenstam won the 1991 NCAA Championship trophy while playing for the University of Arizona.

Annika raises her 1995 U.S. Open trophy. She also won the U.S. Open in 1996 and 2006.

Sand flies as Annika chips out of a bunker during the 2001 LPGA Standard Register PING golf tournament at Moon Valley Country Club in Phoenix, Arizona. Annika became the first woman to break sixty in a professional round during this tournament.

Annika lines up a putt while her friend Tiger Woods watches during the 2001 Lincoln Financial Group Battle at Big Horn exhibition match.

In 2003 the crowd at the Bank of America Colonial, a men's golf tournament, cheers for Annika. Annika was the first woman in fifty-eight years to compete in a PGA event.

Annika celebrates after sinking a birdie putt on the 11th hole at the Skins Game in 2003. By winning the hole, she made $50,000.

Annika stands in front of newcomers Michelle Wie *(left)* and Paula Creamer *(right)* at the awards ceremony for the 2005 McDonald's LPGA Championship. Annika won the tournament, Wie finished second, and Creamer tied for third.

Annika beams as she receives the Best Female Athlete award at the 2005 ESPY Awards.

Annika putts for a birdie during her singles match in the final round of the 2005 Solheim Cup.

Annika hits a tee shot during the playoff round at the 2006 U.S. Women's Open. She went on to win the tournament by four strokes.

With one streak over, there was only one thing for Annika to do—start another one. After the turn, when Annika went back to the first hole to complete the course, she birdied the first hole. Her seven-iron tee shot on the par-three second hole landed twenty-two feet away from the cup. Calmly Annika hit a perfect putt for the birdie. "It was a tricky line, up then down," she said. "When that went in, I said, 'This is just my day.'" The third hole was no match for the red-hot Annika. Yet another birdie left her at eleven shots under par for the day. Annika showed no sign of letting up. Every tee shot hit the fairway. All her approaches landed on the green. Moon Valley's rough, its bunkers, and its water hazards were never a threat.

On the par-four fourth hole, Annika tapped in an 18-inch birdie putt. She had birdied twelve out of thirteen holes! Word of Annika's once-in-a-lifetime round began to buzz around Moon Valley. The gallery grew larger and larger. On the next hole, a par three, Annika missed a nine-foot birdie putt and settled for a par. After she two-putted for pars on each of the next two holes, it looked like her spell had been broken. "I made such an incredible start, and it was such fun, to put it mildly," she said. "By the end, I started to get very nervous."

An important record was still within sight, however. Annika could become the first woman to shoot under 60 in a professional round. On the par-five 8th, she stayed aggressive. After a strong drive down the center of the fairway, she decided to take a risk and go for the green in two. "Annika has a pure, intrinsic drive to excel," said Pia Nilsson. "She doesn't get in her own way."

McNamara handed her a long iron, and Annika hit the ball perfectly. The ball came to rest on the green, twenty feet from the hole. With a chance for an eagle, Annika took her time. She lined up the putt, pulled the putter back, and took the stroke. It was a difficult putt, but Annika came within eight inches of making it. She tapped in her birdie to go to –13 with one hole remaining. A par or better would put her in the record book.

The final hole wasn't easy. With water on the left and bunkers on the right, the narrow par-four 9th was one of the course's toughest. "I was so nervous I was shaking playing the last hole," Mallon said. "You have to appreciate when a fellow competitor shoots close to perfection."

Calmly Annika stroked her drive right down the center of the fairway. Her approach shot was picture-perfect, stopping nine feet from the pin. She slipped the birdie putt just past the hole, but the record was still hers if she could sink the par. Annika stepped to her ball and looked at the immense crowd that had gathered. She smiled and tapped her heart, then tapped in the putt. She had done it! She was the first woman ever to break 60 in a professional round! Annika pumped her fist, turned, and jumped into McNamara's arms.

> **❝***She pushes herself and challenges herself so much that anything is possible.***❞**
>
> —RACHEL TESKE, LPGA GOLFER

While some wondered if the perfect playing conditions were the reason behind Annika's superb play, her fellow golfers knew better. "The way she was playing, I thought she probably could have shot 57," said Webb. "I don't think this course played that easy because the greens were so firm." David Duval, a PGA player who had shot 59 at the Bob Hope Chrysler Classic in January 1999, was all too familiar with the doubters. "They were saying those same things about me," he said. "They're always going to say that. But it's all relative to the other scores, isn't it?"

The sports world was buzzing with news of Annika's historic round. The LPGA hadn't received so much attention in a long time. Annika's accomplishment helped show many people that men weren't the only golfers capable of exceptional achievements. "As far as the quality of golf, it has always been there," Mallon said. "But we needed to get that message beyond our fans and to the general public. And when Annika shoots 59, that helps."

The significance of the accomplishment was not lost on Annika. "I think it shows [women] can play," she said. "There's some very good scoring out there and I wish people can see that. They might say we're not playing at 7,000 yards, but you still have to get the ball in the hole. And I think the girls out here, we do a good job of that."

Annika soaked up the moment, but she knew she still had unfinished business. She still had a tournament to win. In the third round, her hot play continued as she moved to an almost unheard of 23 under par. But twenty-three-year-old Se Ri Pak was playing almost as strongly. After a 62 on Saturday, the young South Korean was just three strokes back, at –20. It was the first time in LPGA history that two players had been 20 under or better after 54 holes.

It's not how good your good shots are. It's how good your bad shots are.

—Annika Sorenstam

Mentally and physically exhausted, Annika entered play on Sunday determined to hang on to her lead. But Pak wouldn't go away. When Pak moved into a tie with four holes left, it appeared Annika's record-setting weekend might not be good enough for a victory.

But Annika showed everyone why she was still the best. With the pressure on, Pak stumbled, bogeying the 15th hole.

Annika quickly capitalized on the youngster's mistake, sinking a seventeen-foot birdie to take a two-stroke lead. This time, she held on to it. In a fitting cap to a fabulous weekend, Annika finished at 27 under par—yet another LPGA record.

A familiar face joined Annika for her round on Sunday—Colin Cann. Cann had been Annika's caddie for years before he became Pak's caddie. None of what he witnessed in Phoenix came as a surprise. "Annika is the best player in the world, man or woman, from 120 yards and in," Cann said. "Her short irons are so good. She hasn't been the number one money winner for two years, and she wants it back." Soon, everyone would be reminded that when Annika had a goal in her sights, she almost always made it a reality.

Chapter Seven

Back in the Saddle

Annika Sorenstam was once again the toast of women's golf. But some people considered her manner on the golf course boring, even robotic. "People want to mold me into Nancy Lopez," she said. "She's a great example of the perfect athlete: somebody who can perform, who smiles, who has charisma. You name it, she has it. I would love to have what she has. Hopefully, I have other qualities. I do what I do. I love what I do. I try to make women's golf as popular as possible."

Real estate mogul Donald Trump played in a pro-am tournament (an event in which amateurs and professionals play together) with Annika. Afterward, someone asked him if the thirty-year-old star could do more to sell herself as a celebrity. "That wouldn't be Annika," Trump answered. "Her whole thing is to be the best golfer she can be. That's what motivates her. She's not interested in anything that gets in the way."

More focused than ever, Annika headed into the first major of the 2001 season looking to follow up her historic win at Moon Valley with her first win in a major in five years. She didn't get off to a good start, however. Annika caught a cold at the beginning of the week. She was still sick on Thursday as the Nabisco Championship got under way. Annika felt miserable, but it didn't show in her play. After the first three rounds, she was tied for second, just one shot behind leader Rachel Teske. Annika's competitive nature shined through in the final round, and she simply refused to lose. As she walked up the 18th fairway, she had a comfortable three-stroke lead. Annika sank a twenty-five-foot birdie, breathed a sigh of relief, and then did what all other winners of the tournament had done in the past— she ran to a nearby lake and jumped in! Annika flashed a huge smile and tossed her visor into the air in celebration.

Her drought in the majors was over at last. With the victory, Annika became the first woman in thirty years to win three consecutive LPGA events, including a major.

If the spotlight had been bright after her historic 59, it became positively blinding after her Nabisco Championship win. Annika was on the cover of *Golf World*. ESPN made her its top story. One couldn't pick up a golf magazine without seeing her face, thanks to numerous ads placed by Callaway, one of her sponsors. She also starred in her first television ad that year.

Annika loves sports, especially basketball. Her favorite team is the National Basketball Association's Sacramento Kings.

The attention was nice, but Annika needed a breather. She took the next couple of weeks off to recharge her batteries. Some wondered if she was making a mistake, stopping right when she was playing her best golf. Annika knew better, however. She simply didn't want to burn out. Long ago she had learned the value of pacing herself. She knew what she needed to succeed at the highest level.

Energized and refreshed, Annika rejoined the Tour at the LPGA Office Depot tournament in Los Angeles. After the first two rounds, it seemed perhaps the doubters were right. Annika looked rusty, falling ten strokes behind leader Pat Hurst. On Sunday, however, Hurst fell apart on the back nine. Meanwhile, Annika and playing partner Mi Hyun Kim were tearing up the Wilshire Country Club course. Annika roared out of the gate with three birdies on the front nine. The highlight was a thirty-five-foot birdie putt on the 4th hole. Birdies on holes 10, 12, and 16 put her in front, but she lost a stroke on 17 when her tee shot was too strong. On hole 18, Annika hit a seven iron off the tee within twelve feet of the pin, then made birdie. "Last year, I would not have made that putt on 18 in regulation, and this year I made it," she said. "It's just being confident with my putter. I've practiced a lot."

Meanwhile, Kim's score of 65 set a course record and left her tied with Annika at six under. Both she and Annika waited forty-five minutes in the clubhouse for Hurst to finish. Hurst had a chance to win on the par-three 18th hole. She needed a birdie for the title and a par to force a three-way playoff. But she sent her tee shot into the front bunker. Her second shot left her with a 15-foot putt for par. She missed. Her 77 left her at five under, one shot behind Annika and Kim.

❝ *She's the best. She's the epitome of integrity and class. She's truly great.* ❞
—GOLFING LEGEND ARNOLD PALMER

On the first playoff hole, Annika's experience and coolness under pressure paid off. Kim sent her tee shot over the 18th green and beyond a back bunker. She had played three shots when Annika calmly made her par for the victory. She had won four tournaments in a row, tying the LPGA record. Coming back from ten strokes down in the final round also set a record for largest comeback in Tour history. "It's unbelievable," Annika said. "I don't know what I've done to deserve all this. It's got to be destiny."

In May Annika won the Chick-fil-A Charity Championship—again in a playoff. On the second extra hole, Sophie Gustafson hit her tee shot into the water. Annika capitalized on her opponent's mistake, tapping in her par for the trophy.

Annika's play gave fans the impression that she simply could not lose. But golf is a difficult game, and Annika suddenly hit a dry spell. She played solidly during the next three months, but rivals such as Webb and Pak got hot. After Pak won the British Open in August, she took over first place on the money list. But Annika won the Montreal Canadian Women's Open in August, putting her back on top of the money list. In October Annika and Pak dueled in the finals of the Cisco World Ladies Match Play Championship in Chiba, Japan. Annika edged out Pak by a single hole for the win.

Annika finished the season on a high note, taking the Mizuno Classic in November. She had eight wins in 2001, and she finished second six times. The thirty-one-year-old had earned more than $2 million and was the first woman to earn more than $7 million in her career. After two long years, she was again the Rolex Player of the Year. Still, a close loss to Webb at the Tyco/ADT Tour Championship in November bothered Annika. While others might have basked in the glory of a record-setting year, Annika spent the winter thinking about what she could do to improve.

To most golf fans, it seemed almost impossible that Annika could get better. But Annika knew she could. She kicked off the 2002 season with a victory at the Takefuji Classic, then finished second to Rachel Teske at the PING Banner Health Open. She won her fourth major in March, defending her title at the Kraft Nabisco Championship. In her next eight tournaments, Annika won four times. At the Kellogg-Keebler Classic, her 11-stroke margin of victory tied the record for the best in Tour history. "If you watch her walk down the fairway, she walks differently," said her personal trainer, Kai Fusser. "Her chest is up . . . there is a confidence there."

 Annika loves cats. She has a cat tattoo, which she says represents her feistiness.

Annika was far and away the best golfer in the LPGA and many expected her to win her favorite tournament—the U.S. Open. While Annika stayed close all weekend, she never found her way to the top of the leaderboard. Juli Inkster took the title with a spirited 66 on Sunday. Annika finished second, two strokes behind Inkster. She was disappointed. But feeling sorry for herself was out of the question.

In July Annika missed the cut at the British Open. But again, she refused to sulk. If anything, she used the stumble as motivation. In the following three weeks, Annika cruised to three wins, giving her nine on the season. Mickey Wright had set the LPGA record for the most victories in a year—thirteen—in 1963. This milestone became Annika's main focus. She defended her title at the Mizuno Classic in November, firing a sparkling 15 under par. But Wright's official record was out of reach when the last tournament of the year rolled around. Unfazed, Annika eked out a close win over Rachel Teske at the ADT Championship for her eleventh LPGA victory of the season.

The win was classic Annika. With two holes left, she led Teske by a single stroke. The 17th hole was a par three surrounded by water. Annika chose a seven iron and hit a perfect shot three feet from the hole. She knocked home the birdie to push her lead to two. On the same hole, Teske scored a double bogey from which she couldn't recover. She finished three strokes behind Annika, who shot a –13.

While she had fallen short of Wright's Tour record, Annika had tied the record for most total wins in a season with thirteen, thanks to victories in Australia and Sweden. Wright had won her thirteen titles in thirty-three starts in 1963. Annika won hers in twenty-four starts. It was another impressive achievement in what was already an amazing career.

 In the winter of 2002–2003, Annika pursued her love of cooking by working in the kitchen at Lake Nona Country Club. The Golf Channel even televised some of Annika's food-related adventures.

If any questions remained as to who was the best woman's golfer in the world, Annika put them all to rest in 2002. Her scoring average of 68.70 shattered her own record, and she earned more than $2.8 million. The extraordinary display was not lost on her rivals—especially her biggest one. "Last year, Annika had a couple of lulls," said Karrie Webb. "But this year, with the exception of missing the cut at the British Open, she contended in almost every event. I don't know where she finds the motivation to be pumped up that much every week."

Chapter Eight

Not Just
a Man's World

Coming into 2003, thirty-two-year-old Annika Sorenstam had made more money than anyone in LPGA history. She'd earned player of the year honors five times. She'd won four majors. She had rewritten the Tour record book. But Annika still wanted to accomplish more. She had always wanted to compete against men. She was curious to see how she measured up.

Annika started the 2003 season blazing hot, finishing in the top five in her first five tournaments. By this time, golf fans were used to Annika's domination. Her stellar performances were no longer all that newsworthy. But Annika made her way back into the spotlight when tournament sponsors asked her to compete at the Bank of America Colonial in May.

The Colonial wasn't an unusual tournament. It was prestigious, but it wasn't a major. The important thing was that the Colonial was an event on the men's PGA Tour.

Annika excitedly accepted the invitation. Almost immediately, the news of her acceptance was the talk of the sporting world. Though PGA rules did not bar women from competing, 1945 was the last time that a woman had competed in a PGA tournament. Everyone seemed to have an opinion, even people who didn't care about golf. Reaction was mixed among fans and the media. Some thought it was great for the sport, men's and women's alike. Many praised Annika for breaking new ground for women. Others, however, thought women should stay in their place—namely, on the LPGA Tour.

Some PGA players spoke out against the decision to let Annika play, including Vijay Singh. Ranked number seven in the PGA, Singh said, "She doesn't belong here. . . . What is she going to prove?" Singh said. "She's the best woman golfer in the world, and I want to emphasize 'woman.' We have our Tour for men, and they have their Tour."

Scott Hoch said that he hoped Annika performed well. But he added, "Most guys hope . . . what comes out of this is that she realizes she can't compete against the men." The Colonial's defending champion, Nick Price, also weighed in. He said Annika's invitation was just a publicity stunt.

Other men, however, welcomed Annika's presence. Phil Mickelson, ranked number four on the PGA, believed Annika had more than earned her chance. "Guys who are having a tough time with this are thinking this is the men's Tour," Mickelson said. "It's not. It's the best Tour, for the best players in the world."

Babe Zaharias

Before Annika's historic start at the Colonial, Texan Mildred "Babe" Zaharias was the last woman to play in a men's tournament. She competed at the Los Angeles Open in 1945. An outstanding athlete, Zaharias also won two gold medals and one silver in track-and-field events at the 1932 Olympics. In 1935 she picked up golf and won seventeen straight amateur victories, a feat that has never been equaled. In 1950 Zaharias completed the Grand Slam, winning all three majors (the sport didn't yet have a fourth major). When ESPN compiled its list of the Fifty Top Athletes of the Twentieth Century, Zaharias was the highest-ranked woman, coming in at number ten.

For her part, Annika refused to add fuel to the fire. In the days leading up to the tournament, she remained gracious and positive. She showed that as a person as well as an athlete, she was pure class. "I'm looking for ways to get better . . . and now I get an opportunity to play against the best men in the world," she said. "I figured this was really testing me and really pushing me to work harder."

Pia Nilsson remained a trusted friend in those difficult days leading up to the Colonial. She maintained that Annika was not out to upset anyone. "Annika has made it clear, this is not about trying to prove that women are better than men," Nilsson said. "She's interested in testing herself, stretching her limits and becoming a role model for the future, for young girls to come, and to take on challenges."

With a storm of controversy swirling around her, Annika remained remarkably calm. Her composure came as no surprise to those who know her best. "Annika is not worried about the golf," Nilsson said. "She said, 'Pia, the worst thing that could happen is that I learn something.' I told her, 'Don't ever let anyone take that away from you.'"

The Colonial took place at a course in Fort Worth, Texas. The course is nicknamed "Hogan's Alley" because golf legend Ben Hogan won there five times. If Annika wanted a challenge, she would certainly get it. The course featured small, fast greens. Annika couldn't hit the ball as far off the tee as most of the men, so she would have to rely on her accuracy. She also knew her short game would be key. She spent a lot of time in practice working on her pitching and putting.

In the past, Annika had received other invitations to play in a PGA tournament. She chose the Colonial because she felt it was best suited to her skills. Hogan's Alley is longer than most

LPGA courses but is considered short by PGA standards. The course rewards accurate shot-making, not brute strength.

 The media and fan attention surrounding Annika at the Colonial was so intense that she hired Tiger Woods's security team.

When the time came to tee off on the first hole, Annika was nervous. But she was determined to have fun. "If you face your scariest moment in public—on national TV—and survive, you're bound to be stronger and happier," she said. With the world watching, Annika smacked her tee shot down the center of the fairway. The gallery erupted in a huge cheer. It was clear that the fans were behind her.

Annika's playing partners were far from household names on the PGA Tour. But Aaron Barber and Dean Wilson tried to make Annika feel at ease, helping calm her nerves with friendly conversation. Wilson even wore a "Go, Annika" pin. A relaxed Annika soon showed why she deserved to be where she was. She scored par on the first three holes. On the par-three 13th, her fourth hole of the day, Annika made a little personal history. After her six iron off the tee had landed just off the backside of the green, she sank the fifteen-foot putt for her first PGA birdie.

Although it was her only one of the day, she kept her mistakes to a minimum. A pair of bogeys was the only blemish on a very respectable round of 71, one stroke over par.

Riding the momentum of her first round, Annika started strong on Friday. A nine iron on the second hole left her with an eight-foot birdie, which she made to move to even par for the tournament. However, the pressure began to wear on her. She badly wanted to reward the faith and support so many fans had showed her. As a result, she seemed to try to be perfect on every shot. A run of five bogeys in eight holes sealed her fate. She finished the round with a 75 and missed the cut by four strokes. For the tournament, she tied for ninety-sixth place, ahead of eleven golfers.

After her final putt on the 18th hole dropped into the cup, Annika took her ball and threw it to a fan. The crowd let her know just how they felt about her performance. With the loudest ovation of the week exploding around her, an incredibly moved Annika shed tears of joy. "Give her five more tournaments, she could make a cut," said golfer Esteban Toledo.

In the end, Annika got her wish. She learned a lot about her game and how she stacked up with the best in the world. "In many instances, I used the same club as the guys for my second shot. Unfortunately, I can't spin the ball like the guys do—that takes brute strength," she said. "Still, I had my fair share of birdie opportunities throughout the two days I played." She also brought attention to women's golf and gained thousands of new fans.

A Tip from Tiger

In 2003 Annika was practicing with Tiger Woods. She noticed Tiger was using only one of his wedges for chip shots instead of different clubs for different distances. Tiger showed her how he adjusted his swing depending on how far he wanted to hit the ball. Annika started using only one wedge as well and credits the tip with improving her short game.

When asked if she'd ever accept another invitation to play against the men, Annika said no. In her heart and in her mind, she'd accomplished just what she set out to do. Though she hadn't made the cut, she'd shown a great deal of dignity and courage.

The following week, Annika returned to the women's Tour. She shot a first-round 62 on her way to victory in the Kellogg's-Keebler Classic. In June she won the fifth major of her career at the LPGA Championship. At the U.S. Open, Annika started slowly. But a third-round 67 put her within striking distance of the leaders. On Sunday she just missed forcing a four-person playoff, finishing one shot off the pace.

While disappointed about not winning the U.S. Open, Annika was pleased with her overall play in the majors. Throughout her career, she had won every major except one: the British Open. When she headed across the Atlantic Ocean in July, she was filled with confidence.

GRAND SLAM

The Grand Slam is when someone wins all four of golf's major championships in the same calendar year. The career Grand Slam refers to someone who has won all four major championships, but not in the same year.

At the Royal Lytham & St. Annes Golf Club in northwest England, Annika and Se Ri Pak added another chapter to their growing rivalry. The two battled back and forth during the final round. With fifty bunkers (sand traps) on the last three holes, Royal Lytham doesn't leave room for error. Unfortunately for Pak, one of Annika's top skills is her course management. "It means knowing where to hit the ball and where not to hit it," she said. "It's knowing what shots you're comfortable hitting, and which angle will give you the best shot into the green. It's knowing when to be aggressive and when not to be, and always thinking one shot ahead."

The pair was tied at 10 under heading to the 18th tee. The British Open would come down to who would make the last mistake. Pak was the first to tee off, hitting her ball into a fairway bunker. Annika answered with a perfect drive, calling it one of the best she had ever hit. For her second shot, Annika used a wedge. She hit a beautiful shot, and the ball came to rest just twelve feet from the flag. All the pressure was on Pak. But the South Korean could not recover from her tee shot and settled for a bogey. When Annika sank her par putt, the crystal trophy—and the career Grand Slam—was hers!

At thirty-two, Annika had won every major tournament at least once. She was the sixth player in LPGA history to achieve the feat. It was yet another outstanding accomplishment in a truly impressive career. "I felt the pressure, but then on the other hand, I felt this is what it's all about, to play in a major championship, where you have to perform, and it was a great feeling," she said. "Now, I'm here, sitting here with a trophy, this is what I wanted for so long."

Annika added to her career victory total at the Safeway Classic. On the way, she made more history, becoming the sixth player to shoot back-to-back eagles. In October she was inducted into the LPGA Tour Hall of Fame. "Acceptance into the Hall of Fame means that I have gained approval from those I deeply respect," she said. "I'm a little overwhelmed at achieving this so quickly in my career, however, I'm very honored to be a part of this elite group."

In November Annika won her third-consecutive Mizuno Classic, firing a blistering 24 under to set a record for a 54-hole tournament. She led the European team to victory at the Solheim Cup, winning four matches. And, in a fitting conclusion to an unforgettable year, the thirty-three-year-old became the first woman to compete in the Skins Game.

The Skins Game isn't an official tournament. Held over Thanksgiving weekend, it is an exhibition in which players compete for prize money on each individual hole. (The winner of each hole earns a skin, which is worth a set amount of money. If a hole is tied, its skin carries over to the next hole.)

Annika faced off against Fred Couples, Phil Mickelson, and Mark O'Meara—three of the biggest names on the PGA Tour. She showed once again why she was one of the world's top golfers—man or woman. She picked up five skins and finished second, earning $225,000. She also hit the shot of the match. On the ninth hole, Annika pulled her tee shot into the rough left of the fairway. Knowing she had no chance of winning the hole with a birdie, she decided on an interesting strategy. "I figured my best chance for eagle was to land my approach in the left greenside bunker and hole it from there," she said.

When Annika hit her seven-wood into the wrong bunker—one 40 yards short and to the right of the green—her situation didn't look good. The bad shot didn't change her plan, however. Using her sand wedge, Annika hit the ball cleanly, barely touching the sand. The ball landed on top of a ridge, bounced a few times, and rolled toward the hole. When the ball rattled into the cup, Annika had picked up four skins and a cool $175,000.

Everyone was amazed. Fred Couples called it the perfect shot. Annika called it "a shot I won't forget." It was a wonderful way for Annika to cap off a memorable season.

Chapter Nine

No End in Sight

Entering 2004 thirty-three-year-old Annika Sorenstam's stature off the course continued to grow. She signed on as a spokesperson with Upper Deck, a trading-card manufacturer. She was the first female athlete to sign with the company.

Annika kicked off the LPGA season in March with a two-stroke win at the Safeway International. The first major came in April, at the Kraft Nabisco Championship. Annika never found a groove and finished tied for thirteenth, a distant eight strokes behind winner Grace Park.

Annika quickly recovered, winning the Office Depot Championship at El Caballero Country Club in Tarzana, California. Her victory there was the fiftieth of her career. She celebrated with cake, which she shared with tournament workers and reporters. After taking the Corning Classic in New York, Annika headed to her second major of the season, the LPGA Championship.

Annika stormed out to a lead after the first round. But then a storm of a different sort—heavy rains—forced the second round to be canceled. Annika spent the day in her hotel room, relaxing and watching movies. The rainout meant she would have to play thirty-six holes on Sunday.

For much of the day, Annika's play was decent but nothing special. Slowly, her six-stroke lead dwindled to two. But Annika fought back. On the 12th hole, she sank a 40-foot putt for birdie. On the 16th, she made a miraculous save. After hitting her tee shot way off course, she had to play down the fairway of the 11th hole, which was nearby. Amazingly, she birdied the hole. Annika cruised to a three-stroke win, finishing at 13 under.

Annika faced several defeats in July. At the U.S. Open, she lost by two strokes to Meg Mallon. At the Ladies' Masters, Wendy Doolan came from behind to take the lead on the front nine. Annika made a charge of her own on the back nine, but she couldn't catch Doolan. The one-shot loss was agonizing and seemed to affect Annika's play at the British Open, where she came in a distant 13th.

In the last six events of the season, Annika rebounded with four wins. In November, she earned her fourth-straight victory at the Mizuno Classic, tying Laura Davies's record for most-consecutive wins in one tournament. In the final tournament of 2004, the ADT Championship, she and Christie Kerr treated the gallery to a classic matchup. On Sunday, the pair battled on the back nine. Annika sank a clutch putt on 16 to tie Kerr, then barely missed a birdie putt on 18 that would have given her the win. Unfazed, Annika took victory on the first hole of sudden death when Kerr plunked her drive into the water.

❝I don't think people realize how hard it is to do what Annika has done the last six years. She's been a dominating force on our Tour and I think she's the most underappreciated athlete there is. I aspire to have the kind of success that she's had.❞

—LPGA GOLFER CHRISTIE KERR

All in all, 2004 was another outstanding year for Annika. In eighteen LPGA starts, she earned eight wins and seven top-ten finishes. For the seventh time in her career, she was Rolex Player of the Year, tying Kathy Whitworth for the most in LPGA history. And she broke her 2002 record for lowest scoring average.

Despite her late run of success, Annika's off-season was difficult. In December, she separated from her husband, David. Two months later, she filed for divorce. The eight-year marriage was over. When the 2005 season began, golf fans wanted to see how this change would affect the famously unflappable Swede.

Annika started the year with impressive wins at the MasterCard Classic and the Safeway Classic. At the Safeway Classic, she found herself four strokes down with three holes to play. Rising star Lorena Ochoa was in the driver's seat after a birdie on the 15th hole, but she lost three strokes with a double bogey on 16 and a bogey on 17. Annika forced a playoff on the par-five 18th hole. After hitting what she called one of the best shots of her life to reach the green in two shots, she tapped in a birdie. On the first extra hole, Ochoa hit her tee shot into a lake and Annika made her par for the win. She then won at the first major of the year, the Kraft Nabisco Championship. Dating to 2004, she had won five starts in a row, tying Nancy Lopez's LPGA record.

 In 2005 Annika earned female athlete of the year honors at ESPN's ESPY Awards. Sorenstam's victory gave her seven career ESPYs, moving her past baseball player Barry Bonds into second on the all-time list. With fifteen, only Tiger Woods has won more.

Annika won two of her next five events, the Chick-fil-A Charity Championship and the ShopRite LPGA Classic. Heading into the second major of 2005, the McDonald's LPGA Championship, every aspect of her game was at its peak.

Annika followed a first-round 68 with a score of 67 in her second round. She cruised to an eight-stroke win, shooting a sparkling 15 under for her ninth major. In addition, she became the first player in LPGA history to win the same major in three consecutive years.

When Annika isn't shattering other people's records, she's breaking her own. In 2005 she became the fastest golfer to reach the $1 million mark in season earnings. In just six events, she erased the record of eight she'd set in 2003 and 2004.

"Right now I want to absorb this," she said afterward. "This is a wonderful feeling and I'm very proud for what I've done. I want it to settle in my heart."

Some fans might think that nothing could surprise Annika after more than ten years on the Tour. But she continued to be stunned by her performances. "I feel like I'm just a little girl from Sweden that came over here to follow my dreams and hope to win a few golf tournaments. When I look at my bio in the LPGA book, I get overwhelmed, definitely. I just feel like sometimes, have I really done this? Is it really true?" she said.

At the McDonald's LPGA Championship, fifteen-year-old Michelle Wie finished second. Another young star, Paula Creamer, also played impressively. As a fan of the game, Annika knew she was watching the future of women's golf. "I felt like when I came out here as a rookie, I was the future, and now I'm seeing another generation. The Tour is in really good hands; it's fun to see," she commented.

Annika claimed her sixth Vare Trophy in 2005. She also took home her eighth Rolex Player of the Year Award, more than any player in LPGA Tour history.

As powerful as Annika was during the first part of the year, she suddenly cooled off. In the next four months, she managed just one win. Then, at the season's close, she once again caught fire, rattling off three victories in her final four starts. Her win in November at the Mizuno Classic in Japan made history, moving her past male golfers Gene Sarazen, Walter Hagen, and Tiger Woods as the only golfer to win the same tournament five times in a row. The LPGA certainly had some shining young stars, but Annika was proving that the old guard was still a force.

Chapter Ten

Full Circle

Thirty-five-year-old Annika Sorenstam was on a mission in 2006. Over the past twelve years, she had accomplished almost every goal she had set for herself. She had shattered records. She had become the second woman to play in a men's event. She had completed the career Grand Slam. And she was the most famous female golfer in history.

But a decade had passed since she'd last won her favorite tournament, the U.S. Open. Annika's goal for the season was to win that event. In late June, she headed to Newport Country Club in Newport, Rhode Island. On Saturday, Annika's chances were looking good. She was tied for the lead with Jane Park. But the first round had been stopped due to fog, meaning Annika would have to play a grueling thirty-six holes of golf on Sunday instead of the usual eighteen. If she was going to break her ten-year drought, it was going to take one of her best efforts.

Consistency had always been one of Annika's strongest suits. On Sunday it served her well. The inexperienced Park faded quickly. Other golfers stayed in the hunt, including Michelle Wie, veteran Juli Inkster, and old rival Se Ri Pak. But soon Newport's notoriously tricky course took its toll. One by one, the competition began to fall back.

Meanwhile, Annika was her strong, steady self. After the first eighteen holes, she was tied for the lead with Pat Hurst. Over the final eighteen holes, the pair battled back and forth. Annika was down a stroke on the par-four 15th hole, but she refused to surrender.

When Annika drained a difficult twenty-footer on the 16th, she was alone in first place. But it was no time to celebrate. On the par-four final hole, Annika had a great chance for the win. Hurst had come up short of the green on her second shot. She made a great chip out of the rough, leaving her with a short putt for par. But Annika had safely reached the green in two shots. If she could make her twenty-two-foot birdie, the U.S. Open would be hers. Annika calmly lined up her putt and brought her putter back, then forward. The gallery was silent. As the ball moved straight toward the hole, Annika was sure she had victory in her sights. But at the last moment, her ball veered to the right. It caught the lip of the cup and rimmed out. Annika held her head in disbelief. Hurst then made her par putt, sending the tournament into a playoff.

In most golf playoffs, the first player to win a hole wins the match. But at the U.S. Open, the rules are different. Annika and Hurst would have to play a complete eighteen-hole round on Monday to determine the winner. Annika lived for such moments. She knew that she was up for the challenge.

 In her book, *Golf Annika's Way*, Annika lists her five most important life lessons. "They're just as effective in real life as they are on the course," she says.
- Face your fear.
- Learn from everything, good or bad.
- Take one shot at a time.
- Focus on what you can control.
- There are no shortcuts.

When she stepped to the first tee on Monday morning, Annika was confident. Right away Hurst struggled, bogeying the first hole. Meanwhile, Annika was at the top of her game. Again and again, her drives landed in the fairway. Her putting was solid and mistake free. Hurst quickly fell five strokes back. But Annika knew her opponent wouldn't give up.

Sure enough, Hurst settled down. She made eight straight pars on the back nine. But pars weren't good enough—Annika was playing too well. On the final hole, Annika still held a five-stroke lead. Hurst finally got a birdie, but it was too late. Annika tapped in her two-foot par, closed her eyes, and raised her arms in happiness—and relief. Annika was once again U.S. Open champion.

 Through 2006 Annika had won more tournaments in the 2000s than any other golfer, man or woman.

"When I came out early and won my first tournament, [it was the] U.S. Open. And [when] I won back to back, I thought, 'Wow, I can do this.' Now it's been ten years," Annika said. "It's been a long wait, a long road, but along the way I've learned a lot, and this week obviously means a lot to me, to come back the way that I did."

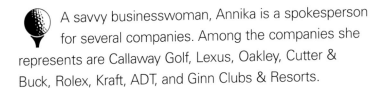

A savvy businesswoman, Annika is a spokesperson for several companies. Among the companies she represents are Callaway Golf, Lexus, Oakley, Cutter & Buck, Rolex, Kraft, ADT, and Ginn Clubs & Resorts.

The rest of 2006 would not be as enjoyable for Annika, however. Mexico's Lorena Ochoa took the Player of the Year Award, as well as the Vare Trophy for lowest scoring average. Annika also finished third on the money list. But Annika's not ready to give up her place at the top without a fight. "I just went back to my coach [Henri Reis] and said, 'Hey, we have to go back to basics; we have to work on my grip, my setup, and everything, just to get back to my consistent swing,'" she said in late 2006. "I do think, to be positive about the whole thing, this is probably good for me. This keeps me motivated, this keeps me on my toes and I continue to work hard and not just take things for granted." After having shown time and time again that disappointment only drives her to new heights, Annika is poised to write the next chapter in her exceptional career.

The Greatest

Before Annika joined the LGPA in 1994, the Tour had never seen a star like her. The Tour has had great players in the past, but none of them captured the public's imagination quite like Annika. As she grew as a person and as a player, she took the game to a new level. People who had never cared much about women's golf were suddenly paying attention. She has changed the face of the sport. Annika's legacy as the greatest golfer in LPGA history is assured.

Just as important as her amazing play is Annika's personality. She is as humble and gracious as any professional athlete in any sport. With each year that passes, she wins over more fans.

While Annika has plenty of years left in her career, she is also planning for a life after professional golf. In 2007 she will host her own tournament on the LPGA Tour—the Ginn Tribute. She is opening the Annika Sorenstam Golf Academy at the

Reunion Resort near her home in Orlando, Florida. (She also has a home in Nevada.) Her coach, Henri Reis, will run the academy. Annika plans on releasing a fitness DVD, and she has successful clothing and jewelry lines. She has combined all of these interests into one company called, simply, "Annika." Her boyfriend, Mike McGee, is managing director of the company. (McGee is familiar with the golf world. He's the son of former PGA Tour player Jerry McGee.)

"I don't know what the future holds," Annika said. "One day, when I can no longer compete at the highest level, I'll leave golf for other things. . . . When that happens, I will miss golf, but I won't regret anything. I'll know I gave the game my all—and I loved every minute of it."

Annika is not ready to retire just yet. In her sights are Kathy Whitworth's eighty-eight career LPGA victories and Patty Berg's record fifteen career majors. At the end of 2006, Annika had sixty-nine LPGA victories and ten career majors. As driven and competitive as she is, Annika may well continue playing until she has added those records to her impressive resume.

Even if she falls short of those goals, her life on and off the golf course has been an amazing story. "Success isn't only about the goal you choose," Annika once said. "It's about the experience, the effort, and the journey."

PERSONAL STATISTICS

Name:

Annika Sorenstam

Nickname:

The Swedish Sensation

Born:

October 9, 1970

Birthplace:

Bro, Sweden

Height:

5' 6"

Residences:

Incline Village, Nevada; and Orlando, Florida

CAREER LPGA TOUR STATISTICS

Year	Majors	Other wins	LPGA wins	Earnings ($)	Money list rank	Scoring average
1994	0	0	0	127,451	39	71.90
1995	1	2	3	666,533	1	71.00
1996	1	2	3	808,311	3	70.47
1997	0	6	6	1,236,789	1	70.04
1998	0	4	4	1,092,748	1	69.99
1999	0	2	2	863,816	4	70.40
2000	0	5	5	1,404,948	2	70.47
2001	1	7	8	2,105,868	1	69.42
2002	1	10	11	2,863,904	1	68.70
2003	2	4	6	2,029,506	1	69.02
2004	1	7	8	2,544,707	1	68.70
2005	2	8	10	2,588,240	1	69.33
2006	1	2	3	1,906,126	2	69.76

GLOSSARY

amateur: an athlete who is not paid for competing in a sport

approach shot: a shot designed to play the ball onto the green and to set up a putt

birdie: one stroke less than par

bogey: one stroke more than par

bunker: a sand trap

chip: a shot from near the green that lofts the ball to roll on the green

cut: the point at which, after a tournament's early rounds, the golfers with the worst scores are eliminated from the competition. Golfers who "make the cut" continue playing.

driver: the golf club that gives a golfer the farthest-possible distance on a shot

eagle: two strokes less than par

fairway: the short-cut grass between the tee and the green

gallery: the crowd gathered to watch a golf event

green: the very short-cut grass surrounding the hole

iron: a club with a narrow, angled club face used for short drives, approach shots, and chips

match: a head-to-head battle between two golfers. In match play, golfers compete to win the most holes.

par: the number of strokes a good golfer should expect to need to get the ball from the tee into the cup

pitch shot: a shot from near the green that is mostly in the air, then rolls a short distance to the green

professional: an athlete who makes a living by competing in a sport

rookie: a first-year professional

rough: the thick grass outside the fairway

Solheim Cup: a tournament that pits top players from the United States and Europe against each other in match play

wood: a golf club with a long shaft and a large club head used for long drives and tee shots

SOURCES

2 Annika Sorenstam, with the editors of *Golf Magazine, Golf Annika's Way* (New York: Gotham Books, 2004), 14.

3 Jerry Porter, "Sorenstam Lives Her Dream," *USA Today*, July 17, 1995, 1-C.

3 Tom Friend, "Sorenstam Outlasts Mallon for U.S. Open," *Austin American-Statesman*, July 17, 1995, D-1.

5 Sorenstam, *Golf Annika's Way*, 14.

6 Ibid., 3.

7 Ibid., 3.

8 Dave Kindred, "Sisters in Arms," *golfdigest.com*, n.d. http://www.golfdigest.com/magazines/index.ssf?/columns/sisters_ijzmba9c.html (January 15, 2007).

9 Sorenstam, *Golf Annika's Way*, 6.

10 Ibid., 7.

12 Ibid., 8.

13 Ibid., 6.

16 Ibid., 11.

16 Debbie Becker, "Sorenstam: LPGA Tour De Force," *USA Today*, July 19, 1997, 1-C.

17 Sorenstam, *Golf Annika's Way*, 11.

17–18 Ibid., 11.

18 Ibid., 12.

24 Ibid., 13.

26 Ibid.

26 Ibid.

34 Ibid., 15.

35 Lisa D. Mickey, "Enjoying the View," *Golf World*, November 1997, 6.

36 "Sorenstam Named Female Athlete of the Year," *golftoday.co.uk*, n.d., http://www.golftoday.co.uk/news/yeartodate/news04/sorenstam19.html (January 15, 2007).

39 Sorenstam, *Golf Annika's Way*, 18.

39 Ibid., 268.

40 "Model of the Week," *askmen.com*, n.d., http://askmen.com/women/models_150/185c_annika_sorenstam.html, (January 15, 2007).

41 Ken Carpenter, "U.S. Open: Source of Inspiration," *thegolfgazette.com*, June 16, 2005, http://www.thegolfgazette.com/modules.php?op=modload&name=News&file=article&sid=2548, (January 15, 2007).

42 Brent Kelley, "Annika Sorenstam," *golf.about.com*, n.d., http://golf.about.com/cs/annikasorenstam/p/annikasorenstam.htm, (January 15, 2007).

43 Mickey, "Enjoying the View," 6.

44 Ibid.

46 Dan O'Neil, "Back on Top Again," *Golf World*, July 1998, 72.

47 Lisa D. Mickey, "Annika Has an Answer," *Golf World*, July 24, 1998, 48.

48 Ibid., 48.

48 Sorenstam, *Golf Annika's Way*, back cover.

49 Ibid., 19.

49 Ibid.

50 Phil Jones, "Eye on the Prize," *cnnsi.com*, April 16, 2001, http://sportsillustrated.cnn.com/thenetwork/news/2001/04/13/annika_sorenstam/ (January 15, 2007).

55 Ibid.

55 Sorenstam, *Golf Annika's Way*, 179.

56 Kelley, "Annika Sorenstam."

57 Sorenstam, *Golf Annika's Way*, 232.

58 Ibid.

58 Mel Reisner, "Sorenstam Shoots LPGA Record 59," *independent.co.uk*, March 17, 2001, http://sport.independent.co.uk/golf/article247938.ece (January 15, 2007).

58 ESPN Golf Online/Associated Press, "Mallon Has Been Witness to LPGA History," *espn.com*, Match 20, 2001, http://espn.go.com/golfonline/Tours/s/2001/0320/1158842.html (January 15, 2007).

59 Lisa D. Mickey, "Just Call Her Mrs. 59!" *golfworld.com*, March 2001, http://www.golf54.com/html/just _call_her_mrs__59.html (January 15, 2007).

59 BBC Sport, "Sorenstam Rewrites Record Book," *news.bbc.co.uk*, March 16, 2001, http://news.bbc .co.uk/sport1/hi/golf/1225804.stm (January 15, 2007).

60 Mickey, "Just Call Her Mrs. 59!"

60 Ibid.

61 Jockbio.com, "Annika Sorenstam: What They Say," *jockbio.com*, n.d., http://www.jockbio.con/Bios/ Sorenstam/Sorenstam_quotes.html, (January 15, 2007).

61 Mickey, "Just Call Her Mrs. 59!"

61 ESPN Golf Online/Associated Press, "Mallon Has Been Witness to LPGA History."

61 Ibid.

62 ESPN Golf Online, "Sorenstam Reaches Golf's Magic Number," *espn.com*, March 21, 2001, http:// espn.go.com/golfonline/Tours/s/ 2001/0316/1156236.html (April 20, 2007).

62 Michael Bamberger, "The Amazing Annika," *Sports Illustrated*, December 2, 2002, 46.

63 Mickey, "Just Call Her Mrs. 59!"

64 Michael Bamberger, "A Woman Among Men," *Sports Illustrated*, February 24, 2003, 62.

64 Ibid.

67 Cnnsi.com, "More Than a Miracle: Sorenstam Rallies for Record-Tying 4th Win in a Row," *cnnsi.com*, April 15, 2001, http://sportsillustrated .cnn.com/golf/news/2001/04/14/ office_depot_ap/ (January 15, 2007).

67 Sorenstam, *Golf Annika's Way*, back cover.

68 Cnnsi.com, "More Than a Miracle: Sorenstam Rallies for Record-Tying 4th Win in a Row."

69 Greg Boeck, "Sorenstam Radiates Confidence on the Fairways," *usatoday.com*, February 12, 2004, http://www.usatoday.com/sports/ golf/2004-02-12-sorenstam -toughest_x.htm (January 15, 2007).

71 Randall Mell, "Annika Sorenstam Employs a Swedish Philosophy to Help Her with Golf, Life," *golf54.com*, November 2002, http://www.golf54.com/html/ sorenstam_employs_swedish_phil .html (January 15, 2007).

73 Jessica Hoffmann, "Annika Sorenstam," *woa.tv*, n.d., http:// www.woa.tv/articles/at _sorenstama.html (January 15, 2007).

73 Jerry Potter, "Singh Says Annika 'Doesn't Belong' on PGA Tour," *usatoday.com*, May 13, 2003, http://www.usatoday.com/sports/ golf/pga/2003-05-12-singh_x.htm (January 15, 2007).

73–74 Ibid.

74 Christine Brennan, "Sorenstam Says All the Right Things," *golf54.com*, May 20, 2003, http:// www.golf54.com/html/sorenstam _says_right_things.html (January 15, 2007).

75 Thomas Bonk, "Sorenstam Tries a Proving Ground," *golf54.com*, May 18, 2003, http://www.golf54.com/ html/sorenstam_tries_a_proving _grou.html (January 15, 2007).

75 Ibid.

76 Sorenstam, *Golf Annika's Way*, 21.

77 Michael Bamberger, "Her Best Shot," *Sports Illustrated*, June 2, 2003, 52.

78 Sorenstam, *Golf Annika's Way*, 73.

79 Ibid., 205.

80 "In Their Own Words: Annika Sorenstam," *The Wire*, August 4, 2003, http://www.golftransactions .com/fivequestions/ sorenstam080403.html (January 15, 2007).

80–81 "Sorenstam and Price Inducted into Hall of Fame," *golfonline.com*, October 20, 2003, www.golfonline .com/golfonline/news/headlines/ 0,,news-tsn_20031020_221513,00 .html (January 15, 2007).

82 Sorenstam, *Golf Annika's Way*, 171.

82 Ibid.

85 LPGA, "News and Notes from Nov. 22, 2004, *lpga.com*, November 22, 2004, http://lpga.com/content _1.aspx?mid=4&pid=3344 (January 15, 2007).

87 LPGA, "Annika in the Press Room," *lpga.com*, June 13, 2005, http:// www.ladieseuropeanTour.com/ content/let_content_interview.php ?Id=3817 (January 15, 2007).

87 Ibid.

88 Ibid.

91 Sorenstam, *Golf Annika's Way*, 21.

92 "ESPN Interview with Annika Sorenstam," *www.uswomensopen .com*, n.d., http://www .uswomensopen.com/2006/news/ interviews/Annika_Sorenstam_07 _03_06_espn.html (January 15, 2007).

93 George White, "Annika's Not Fretting Over 2006," *thegolfchannel .com*, November 16, 2006, http:// www.thegolfchannel.com/core .aspx?page=15104&select=21230 (January 15, 2007).

95 Sorenstam, *Golf Annika's Way*, 21.

95 Ibid., xv.

BIBLIOGRAPHY

Galyean, Gary A. *Golf Rules Illustrated*. New York: Sterling Publishing, 2001.

Hauser, Melanie. *Champions of Women's Golf: Celebrating Fifty Years of the LPGA*. Naples, FL: QuailMark Books, 2000.

Savage, Jeff. *Annika Sorenstam*. Minneapolis: Lerner Publications Company, 2005.

Sorenstam, Annika, with the editors of *Golf Magazine*. *Golf Annika's Way*. New York: Gotham Books, 2004.

Williams, Jackie. *Playing from the Rough: The Women of the LPGA Hall of Fame*. Las Vegas: Women of Diversity Productions, 2000.

WEBSITES

The LPGA Tour's Official Website

http://www.lpga.com

The official site of the LPGA Tour includes player biographies, statistics, live scoring, results, and feature articles.

ESPN.com Golf

http://sports.espn.go.com/golf/index

ESPN.com's golf page features news about past and upcoming golf events, player biographies, statistics, leaderboards, and feature articles.

Golf for Women Magazine

http://www.golfdigest.com/gfw

This magazine is devoted to women's professional golf. It includes feature articles, tips on equipment, and lessons, news, and photos.

INDEX